Wha...
"How...
ON YOUR INCOME
and Hans Jakobi

"Hans, your newest book is going to help thousands of people worldwide have more financial freedom in their lives. You show anyone exactly how to have the true wealth of the world. You teach people correct wealth and success principles; how to have more balance and control in their life, how to have more time with family and how to live life with a passion. Because of your love for life and your love for people, you are exactly the type of person that anyone would want to have as a coach and mentor. On a scale of 1-10, I would rate this book as a 12+"

Wright Thurston
President/CEO International Success Group Inc.,
Author of "How to Earn an Extra $100,000 in Two Years or Less", And "Making It Happen: Getting Rich the 'Wright' Way"
Sandy, Utah, USA

"This book is a goldmine of valuable and powerful money management tools which can be applied immediately. This straightforward and practical book reveals how to manage money better and enjoy a richer life."

Raymond Aaron
Canada's Monthly Mentor™
Toronto, Ontario, Canada

"This book is packed with powerful, practical and easy to understand tools to live a richer and happier life on your present income. What's more, - this book shows you how to increase your current income and how to build real wealth."

Anne Hartley
International Best-Selling Author of
"Financially Free", "Debt Free" and
"The Psychology of Money"
Sydney, NSW, Australia

"If you want to be like most people then don't listen to Hans Jakobi, because he'll teach you not only how to keep more of what you get but to get more of what there is."

W Mitchell CPS CSP CPAE
Santa Barbara, California, USA

"Powerful, practical and persuasive philosophies for people who really want to be genuinely wealthy. If you want to live the lifestyle you dream about, this is must read stuff. Then stop dreaming and start doing! This is the best investment you'll ever make in your future."

Winston Marsh
International Business Authority
Melbourne, Victoria, Australia

"How To Be Rich & Happy On Your Income hits the nail on the head with regards taking responsibility for one's life, finances and happiness. It is the foundation for all success."

Art Berg CSP Professional Speaker
Author, "Finding Peace in Troubled Waters"
& "Some Miracles Take Time"
Highland, Utah, USA

"Your book is easy to read and the 'In Summary' really encapsulates the key points. Thank you for sharing the principles of creating wealth in such a simple, logical form. This book is a 'must read' for every small business owner."

Robyn Henderson ASM APS
Author, International Business Educator
Sydney, NSW, Australia

"Practical advice, presented in an easy to read format…Offers common sense advice to help any individual get started on their personal journey of how to be rich and happy."

Catherine DeVrye
1993/94 Australian Executive Woman of the year
Sydney, NSW, Australia

"The student becomes a teacher. Hans first attended one of my seminars around ten years ago and has been to several more since then. He has implemented what he has learnt to grow his own investment portfolio and now teaches wealth creation strategies to others. His book, How To Be Rich & Happy On Your Income is required reading for anyone committed to increasing the quality of their life. Stimulating and inspiring, it deals with everyday issues in a way that is thought provoking and relevant for today."

Robert Kiyosaki
Professional Investor, Best-selling Author
"Rich Dad, Poor Dad", Teacher,
Phoenix, Arizona, USA

"Fantastic! This is much more than a book about money … it's a book about your life! It shows you step by step how to take control of your life and make it as fun and financially successful as you always dreamed it would be. Inspiring and educational, it's a "must" for everyone to read."

Mark Lengies
Author of "Internet Marketing Secrets"
Kitchener, Ontario, Canada

"This book is indispensable for clear, simple personal development and wealth building ideas. In every chapter you will gain practical guidelines for developing prosperous attitudes and inspiring immediate actions to truly master your life and create wealth."

David Wolrige
Public Accountant,
Sydney, NSW, Australia

"How To Be Rich & Happy On Your Income is a practical, easy-to-read, nuts and bolts book. I particularly like the section on relationships and also how to teach your children about money. This is a useful, positive and profitable book to read."

Cyndi Kaplan
Author of the best selling book
"There's A Lipstick In My Briefcase"
Sydney, NSW, Australia

"Hans draws on his own extensive experience and shows how creating wealth really has to do with relationships, lifestyle and personal fulfillment as well as money (allowing freedom of choice). It is an honest and comprehensive book which allows you to learn the beliefs and practical steps to have the life you want and deserve."

Gary Russell
Success Coach
Canberra, ACT, Australia

"Hans has created a truly delightful asset with this work. It would be impossible for a reader not to gain an insight into the mindset necessary for the wealth creation process. The difference between poverty and plenty is nothing more than some simple knowledge, multiplied by time and triggered by some catalyst. This book is a smorgasbord of catalysts.

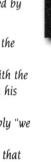

This should not be surprising as the subject material of the book is not hypothetical but is the result of real life application. Some years ago Hans associated himself with the Hudson Institute which publishes my own books. Given his extremely high level of knowledge of the wealth creation process, I asked of him his reason. The answer was simply "we never stop learning". I hold an enormous delight in the qualities of the species human and Hans has confirmed that faith. This confirmation is not in just the display of excellent qualities but in having a genuine desire to elevate others to a better quality of life.

Hans was good enough to present on behalf of the Hudson Institute because of his desire to communicate both the message and the means. The motivation for Hans is not ego but a real desire to add to the human condition. Hans is motivated by his wife, children and the general community and his contribution will allow many to warm themselves in the financial heat generated by this work.

I congratulate Hans with the utmost sincerity and watch with restrained excitement for the ripple or wave of success that will rightfully accrue to the reader of this work."

Stuart Moore
Author of "How to start with no savings and get rich … *safely*" and "Trading Australian Futures"
Brisbane, QLD, Australia

How To
Be
Rich & Happy
ON YOUR
INCOME

Hans Jakobi

author of

Super Secrets to Wealth,

Super Secrets to Riches

and

How Real Estate Investment
Can Work For You

This book is available at special quantity discounts for bulk purchases for sales promotions, premiums or fundraising. Special books or book excerpts can also be created to fit specific needs.

To discuss your needs, contact the Distribution Manager at

Wealth Dynamics International Pty Ltd,

PO Box 86 Illawong NSW 2234 Australia.

Telephone: (02) 9543 2966

Fax: (02) 9543 5048

Email: wealth@supersecrets.com

Dedication

To my wife, Colette, and our three children who, for more years than I care to count, have stood by my side challenging and encouraging me to nurture that God-given gift of creativity; and also to my mother and father, Pauline and John, for their understanding and love.

I love you all.

On the other hand... spread the ideas around as much as you can!

National Library of Australia
Cataloguing-in-Publication Entry:

Jakobi, Hans, 1953-
How to be rich & happy on your income

Bibliography.
Includes index
ISBN 1 876818 00 X.

1. Finance. Personal - Psychological aspects 2. Money - Psychological aspects. 1. Title

332.024

First Published – May 1998
First Reprinted – July 1998
Second Reprint – August 1998

Illustrated by: Alex Bosi
Printed in Australia by: Australian Print Group, Maryborough, Victoria
Distributed by: Capricorn Link (Australia) Pty Ltd
2A/13 Carrington Rd Castle Hill NSW 2154.
Ph: (02) 9899 8322 Fax: (02) 9899 8211
Cover Design and Typeset by: Michael Shaw

Published by: Wealth Dynamics International Pty Ltd (ACN 081 878 499)
PO Box 86, Illawong, NSW 2234 Australia
Telephone: (02) 9543 2966 Fax: (02) 9543 5048
E-mail: wealth@supersecrets.com
Website: www.supersecrets.com

Acknowledgments

To the many people who have helped and encouraged me in my work and supported me in the writing of this book, thank you. In particular, thank you to–

- Gary Schuller and Toney Fitzgerald for always encouraging me to realise my true potential and to move in the direction of my dreams, even when I didn't think it was possible.

- Stuart Moore for explaining the economic clock to me in an easy to understand fashion and in opening my mind to the potential within all of us to reach financial independence.

- To the following teachers who inspired me, Dr Wayne Dyer, Dr Stephen Covey, Robert Kiyosaki, Raymond Aaron, Barry Black, Bob Proctor, Robert Allen, Anthony Robbins.

- Michael Shaw for your creative ideas for this book, our audio programmes and our ongoing educational seminar programme.

- My parents, John and Pauline Jakobi, for the lessons you have taught me and for the opportunities you provided for me.

- To my children Carina, Michael and Stephanie for your understanding and compassion while I kept unusual hours during the writing of this book, the ideas you contributed and the lessons I learnt through you.

- To my wife Colette for all the typing and reading you have done to see this project through. Thank you for being such a great partner.

- To my mother-in-law Elisabeth Neuens for her help and support when we needed it most.

- To Anne Hartley, for without her support, the writing of this book would not have been possible.

- And to Sandra Dekker Dignam for her proof reading and suggestions.

Introduction

In 1995 I was faced with a personal crisis. I had just sold a distribution business that I had operated for several years with the intention of taking over a food manufacturing plant, but at the last moment the takeover fell through and I was at a loose end. I had been trained as a chartered accountant (my degree is in economics and accounting), and I had worked in accounting practices and my father's business before venturing out on my own. I knew I wanted to work for myself, but at that time I wasn't sure what it was that I wanted to do. This was a pattern that had occurred in my life before and I usually opted for security, by going back to a salaried position. This time however, I decided to do it differently, although I must admit for a time I lost my fire and enthusiasm and felt that I lacked direction.

While I was looking around for opportunities, I took a short-term job selling investment real estate. I have invested in real estate myself for many years and it was something I believed in. However, what I discovered during my short time with this company was that many people were being misled.

The company that I worked for sold investment properties in Queensland and would fly potential investors interstate for a free look at the properties for sale. The clients would be picked up at the airport and then driven to visit the properties. However, what the Queensland salespeople were told to do was to drive a certain route. They could not drive past any billboards advertising other properties, nor real estate agents' offices. In fact the whole presentation was organised so that the unsuspecting client would have no idea of what comparable values were in that area. As most investors came from Sydney, the prices quoted, in comparison to Sydney, appeared to be good value. Most of these properties were sold at around 20 per cent above market value. Many of the salespeople selling these properties were not always aware of this fact. I certainly wasn't.

The clients were encouraged to sign a contract on the day of their visit. Generally they were told that this was the last property available, and most people signed the contract then and there. Under NSW law there is a cooling-off period that allows people to change their mind, but as these contracts were signed in the presence of a Queensland solicitor, no cooling-off period applied. The contract was binding.

The question I have been asked many times since is, how do they get away with it, particularly when banks generally approve the finance? This is when I first began to suspect that all was not what it appeared to be. A common practice was to mortgage the investment property as well as the client's home. I became suspicious when clients with perfectly good credit ratings and the potential to pay off a loan were refused finance. What separated these clients from the ones that were approved was that they already had a substantial mortgage on their home. The clients whose applications were approved easily had a large amount of equity in their property.

Having been trained in accounting and auditing one tends to get suspicious. What I soon realised was that as the banks would have a first mortgage on the investor's home they could draw on this to any value if the investor defaulted. In other words, if the bank held a mortgage of $20,000 on the investor's home and $175,000 was owed on the property, then the bank could claim that amount in a default situation. When clients already had substantial mortgages, the banks (who must have known that these properties are over-priced), did not have as much security and they therefore refused the loan. Some of these investors were then encouraged to take out mortgage insurance to qualify for a loan.

Many unsuspecting investors who had been promised high rents and growth in property values were stuck with white elephants that they could not rent. Eager to get out and cut their losses, some investors decided to sell and sometimes the company that sold them the property in the first place offered to take it off their hands at a considerably reduced price. The company then sold this property again, at inflated values, to the next sucker that came along.

It is not just the naive who are being conned. I know of one family where the father is a property investor and general manager of a large company. He encouraged his 20 year old son to invest his hard-earned savings in property. The son bought a one bedroom unit in Sydney from one of the well-known companies that advertises frequently. His parents checked it out and approved it. Eighteen months later a well-known developer was selling brand new apartments just across the road from the property for $30,000 less than the young man paid for his unit.

Naturally, once I realised what was happening, I left my job immediately. That experience led me to discover my passion. I wanted to be part of the solution and not part of the problem. I wanted to teach the secrets of creating wealth honestly. Wealth to me is more than just money, it encompasses relationships, lifestyle and personal fulfilment as well as money. Money is the tool that provides us with freedom and the luxuries of life. Having discovered my purpose, I set about creating my current business, Wealth Dynamics International Pty Ltd and my purpose is to live and teach the principles of true wealth. Since that time I have developed two home-study programmes, conducted seminars, produced a newsletter and recorded an audio wealth library.

I consider myself a fortunate man to have a great marriage, three wonderful children, to love my work and to have been able to build a substantial asset base for my family and I know it is not luck. It saddens me that our education system does not teach the principles of making money. If we educate children how to master money we would have financially secure people and more efficiently run Governments and businesses within a few decades. Less people would be reliant on Government handouts and charity and we would be able to make a positive contribution to the international economy.

As you read this book you will hear and perceive exactly what you want to hear and perceive, based on your current values, beliefs, prejudices and past experiences.

Sidney Herbert Wood said that the test of an educated person is as follows:

Can I entertain a new idea?
Can I entertain another person?
Can I entertain myself?

This book is based on the idea that you have unlimited resources lying dormant within you just waiting to be developed. The development of these resources will lead to the manifestation of prosperity in your material world. Material wealth is a normal and natural state for all of us to live in. You deserve wealth and the fulfilment of your fondest dreams.

It is my intention in writing this book to share with you much of what I have learned about true wealth.

There may be times when I repeat myself and I do this because we learn by repetition.

I know you can be rich and happy. It is within your power.

Read this book a couple of times. Not once - two or three times. I have found that as we read things over, they start to take on a different meaning. I read somewhere that when you read a good book through the second time you often pick up something you didn't see the first time. Your perceptions have changed because *you* have changed. As you read through this book again, you will start to relate to it a little differently, and you will relate to money differently.

---

*Money gives an appearance of beauty
even to ugliness; but everything
becomes frightful with poverty.*

Boileau

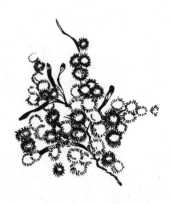

Chapter One

Money is Important

*If money can't buy happiness why is everyone
trying to get it?*

Scott Alexander

**Money will have a greater influence on your life
than almost any other commodity you can think of.**

As I sat on the wharf with my children and fished
whilst on holiday one year, I started a conversation
with an elderly gentleman who was fishing nearby. As
we talked we watched a magnificent cruiser pull out of
the harbour with a merry group of people aboard, obviously looking forward to a day's deep sea fishing. The
old man turned to me with a weary look and said,
"When I had the money, I didn't have the time. Now I
have all the time in the world and I don't have the
money to fish in style". It's a sad reflection of life that
rings true for too many. Unfortunately the statistics
prove that unless you take charge of your life, this
could happen to you.

If you have doubts about how important money is,
then just imagine for a moment how you would func-
tion without money. How would you buy your
groceries each week? Pay your rent? How would you
get around? What would you do if you could not pay
your electricity or phone bill?

The everyday commodities of life that we take for granted such as a roof over our head, TV, telephones, cars and transport are all paid for with money and that money usually comes from some form of work that we do to *make a living*. The problem is that in making a living most people forget about creating a life. Creating a life as well as being rich and happy is what this book is all about.

There may come a time when technology will enable us to eliminate cash but that does not mean that we eliminate the commodity known as money.

These are the facts:

Two-thirds of Australians live from pay cheque to pay cheque until the day they die.

Only 10 per cent of Australians achieve some measure of financial security.

Only 2 per cent manage to achieve real financial freedom.

The chart below clearly demonstrates these facts. The question is, do you want to live this way?

Australian incomes

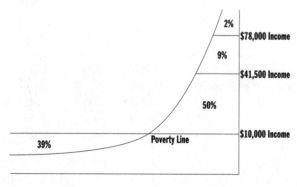

Source: 1996 Census – Australian Bureau of Statistics

Wealth tip:
When you ask, Why does this always happen to me? You become powerless.

Having said all of the above, I am not advocating that you let money run your life. Not surprisingly though, the **lack** of money is what actually rules most people's lives. Let's look at some more facts:

- Fights over money have been cited as the major cause of conflict in marriages.

- Lack of money forces many to remain in jobs that they are less than passionate about and often actively dislike.

- Debt forces others to spend and live a certain way. If you are in debt your choices are no longer your own. Your choices are dictated by your credit providers. Have you ever had to shop at a certain department store because that was the only one where you had available credit on your charge card?

The facts are that most people become locked into jobs, relationships and lifestyles simply because of money, or more appropriately the lack of it. Lack of money, more than anything else, is what restricts personal freedom.

Aged pension recipients by age

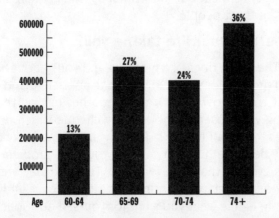

Source: 1996 Census – Australian Bureau of Statistics

Another very important fact is that we are living longer - and the longer you live the more money you are going to need. A 30 year old today can expect to live to about 76-77. Life expectancy increases once you

Wealth tip:
When you ask,
What can I learn?
You become
powerful.

reach 65 and by then you will probably live to about 85. As medical science advances and we are healthier, the odds are in our favour to live even longer.

Money is important

One of the most basic laws governing true financial success is to **love people and use money**, not the other way around. You can enjoy money - respect it and use it but money is merely a tool. Having money won't change you - it will just enhance what you already are. If you are already selfish and greedy, you'll be that way with or without money. If you are mean and fearful you'll remain the same if you have more money. On the other hand, if you are generous and want to share your knowledge and wealth with others, then you can help your children and friends or become a philanthropist. Respect money for all the good it can do. Have good plans for your money. Enjoy money and have a desire for money, but never live your life for money. Money is a tool, a means of exchange. Having money is a lot more fun than always struggling to make ends meet but unfortunately this is the reality of life for most people.

Where is your life taking you?

The alarm rings of a morning and you get out of bed and prepare for work. Do you wake up excited and can't wait to get to work? Or does another day on the job bring you closer to another pay cheque which in turn goes to pay all the bills. Perhaps if you are lucky there may be something left over for you? The problem with this cycle is that it never ends. The next day and the day after that you continue this ritual over and over again. Is this what you want for yourself and your children?

Wealth is when small efforts produce big results. Poverty is when big efforts produce small results.

George Davis M.D.

The fact is that when you work at a job just for money your income is rarely enough. You become locked into a system that is ruled by fear. Your life is ruled by what ifs. What if I lose my job? What if interest rates goes up? What if I can't pay the mortgage or rent on time? What if I take a chance and lose?

Fear is what keeps you in debt. Fear is what keeps you on the same old treadmill but fear does not keep you safe from disaster. Whatever you focus your attention on you attract more of into your life, so it is no wonder then that most people are a slave to money rather than the other way around.

What most people do

Remember that the average person is not rich, in fact the average person knows very little about money management and even less about creating wealth. So when it comes to creating wealth, don't look to the average person for solutions. Your brother, neighbour or work mate are not the best people to go to for advice as they probably know less than you do. Talk to someone who is already wealthy and learn from them. The way to create wealth is to get your money working for you rather than you working for money.

Most people who go to work to make money think it is impossible for them to get started on any type of investment programme. When money is tight they often work harder. Sound familiar? The problem is that there are only so many hours in each day and the harder you work, the more tax you pay. Often you move into a higher tax bracket, your quality of life reduces and you sometimes wonder if it is all worth it. What most people don't realise is that working hard will rarely make you rich. In fact I have come across people who are too busy to make money. Their time is so occupied with activities that they don't take the time to plan, to structure their affairs or to invest. The sooner you divert some of your income into investments, the sooner you'll be able to work less, and the sooner you'll have your money working for you.

There are others who get tired of the rat race and have what Michael Gerber, author of The E Myth,

It is a kind of spiritual snobbery that makes people think they can be happy without money.

Albert Camus

23

describes as an entrepreneurial seizure. One day you decide you want to be your own boss. It's not that having your own business has always been your dream, but you see it as a way to make more money. Sometimes it is, but the statistics prove that for most people it is not. Most businesses fail within the first five years, that is a fact. The problem with an entrepreneurial seizure is that one day you wake up and say to yourself, *What have I done?* Often you find yourself working harder, longer and for less money than you did as an employee.

Some people opt for seeking advice from a financial planner, but the problem is that very few financial planners are interested in seeing you unless you have a reasonable sum of money to invest. There are a few financial advisers that will give you impartial advice for a fee, but they are very few. Most financial planners sell investment products and their income comes from commissions they receive from investment companies. The same applies to insurance salespeople. Although it is not impossible to find someone who has your best interests at heart, you need to be careful taking this route.

It has always amazed me that so many people who are around money all day long really don't understand money and often don't have their own finances under control. So make sure you are dealing with someone who is prepared to demonstrate a successful financial record before you part with your hard earned money.

Sometimes the journey from where you are to where you want to be just seems too hard and too long and that may be the time when you say, I *don't care about money* or, *money isn't important.* But just imagine how you would feel if you lost or were robbed of a large amount of money. Imagine too that you suddenly and unexpectedly came into a substantial sum of money. Wouldn't you be influenced by either of these events?

It's easy to remain mediocre.

Jim Rohn

Whether you like it or not, money plays an important

24

role in our everyday life and if you choose to ignore that fact then you become a statistic.

How close are you to achieving financial freedom?

The following questionnaire was designed as a measure for testing your financial fitness. For each question rate yourself on a scale of 1 to 4 to discover how close you are to achieving financial freedom. The higher you score, the closer you are to achieving that freedom.

The rating scale is as follows: 1 means poor
2 means satisfactory
3 means good
4 means excellent

1. I am free of financial faults.
    This means that you never skip one bill to pay another. You never need to ask for an advance on your salary or commission. Your bank account has a credit balance and you don't go into overdraft. You balance your cheque book regularly and you pay out your credit card and other debts in full every month.

2. I have no problems with my creditors.
    Your wages are not in danger of being garnisheed. There is no likelihood of your property being repossessed. You do not receive calls from creditors. Your credit record is free of blemishes.

3. I am free from overextended debt.
    This means that less than 20 per cent of your personal income goes to service consumer debt. You spend less than you earn.

4. I don't worry about money matters.

5. I don't have any health challenges as a result of financial stress.

6. I don't argue with my spouse/partner about money matters.

7. I have adequate insurance cover for health, trauma, death, disability, loss of income and property insurance.

8. I have three to six months worth of income set aside in savings to cover the unexpected.

9. I always pay myself first. This means saving at least 10 per cent of your income and investing for future benefits.

10. I take an interest in tax planning strategies and am always looking for ways to maximise my tax deductions legitimately.

11. I have an adequate retirement plan in place.

12. I provide a hedge against inflation and capital loss through diversified income producing investments.

Add up your total score _____

How did you score?

If your score is between 12 and 23 you need to seriously devote immediate attention to putting your financial affairs in order. Your state of financial fitness is flawed.

If your score is between 24 and 34 your state of financial fitness is fair. You have a reasonable foundation from which to develop financial freedom by improving your areas of weakness.

If your score is between 35 and 39 you have your financial affairs under control and are doing fine. There are still some areas that can be improved and fine-tuned to take you to the next level.

A score between 40 and 48 is fantastic. You have achieved financial freedom. Congratulations! Please teach others around you how to achieve greater levels of prosperity.

In my opinion you cannot beat self-education. You

Wealth tip:
Everybody retires one day but not everybody retires financially secure. Review your financial plans now.

don't have to become a tax expert but you do need to understand how the system works, how to best manage your money and what your options are. Knowledge is what gives you freedom and acting on that knowledge can make you rich.

For centuries, dating back to the ancient Greeks and Romans, man tried to break the four minute mile. The Romans even had lions chase men to see if they could achieve this feat. It was decided that it was humanly impossible.

One day a young Englishman, Roger Bannister, made the decision that he would break this record. On 6 May 1954 Roger Bannister ran the mile in three minutes 59.6 seconds. He did the impossible. Since that time more than 40 people have broken this record.

The impossible can become the norm when the belief changes.

Remember, the rich don't work for money, their money works for them. Grant yourself permission to have all that your heart desires and if you really want to know, I can show you how to be both rich and happy.

In Summary

1. Acknowledge that money is important and that you need to take responsibility for providing for your own future.

2. Give yourself permission to have all that your heart desires.

3. Acknowledge your current financial position and decide where you would like to be five years from today.

4. Make self-education a priority so that you can make informed choices.

Chapter Two

Breaking Free

Our greatest dreams are never out of reach,
only out of belief.

Wayne Dyer

The biggest obstacles to our achieving what we want lies behind the iron curtain that we have erected in our minds.

On 9 November 1989 the impossible happened and the Berlin Wall was knocked down. Shouts of joy were heard throughout the world as freedom was claimed by East Germans who had been trapped behind the iron curtain since 1961. The Berlin wall represented struggle, hardship, bondage, separation and lack. Suddenly, the restrictions that had applied for 28 years dissolved as the iron curtain crumbled and citizens of former communist strongholds were granted privileges that we in the western world take for granted as our right.

In 1967 my parents, sister and I travelled throughout Europe to Romania, which was then under communist rule, to visit relatives. My grandparents lived in a small village with only a few hundred residents about a day's drive from Bucharest. My father, who had been back to Romania several times since the war ended, stocked up on chewing gum, blue jeans, toilet paper and several other commodities. At the time we did not understand the significance of his actions until we arrived and discovered what real lack was all about. In Romania these goods represented wealth and freedom.

For those of us who have grown up in a western society surrounded by an abundance of goods and choices, it is hard to imagine the different quality of life that these people experienced. The local shop in my grandparents' village received supplies about once every six weeks. Something as basic as butter or toilet paper would be snapped up within one and a half hours of its arrival at the store. Luxury items such as chewing gum were just not available at all. When we went shopping in a large regional town we discovered to our dismay that the supermarkets had mostly empty shelves. My uncle explained that most items were rationed and you could not just walk in and buy what you wanted, that is assuming you had the money in the first place. In those days specific shops were allocated for tourists and these stores carried an abundance of goods at prices too high for the locals, and purchases had to be paid for in foreign currencies. These shops had an abundance of stock while the stores for local residents remained bare.

It was at that time that I became aware that there are vast differences in the way people live. Ordinary everyday items we take for granted as our right can be considered luxuries by others. The freedom to shop and walk the streets is another thing that we take for granted. As visitors to a communist country we had to report to the local police station at various intervals and there were many restrictions placed upon us.

Much of what I have learned about money and creating wealth I have learned from my father. My father gave me the opportunity to experience life under communist rule so that I could understand and appreciate all that we have today. As a boy I believed

Wealth tip:
When you invest your power in money and possessions you risk losing it.

those differences were a direct result of living in a democratic society as opposed to communist rule. However, as an adult, having spent much of my working life as a chartered accountant advising clients on money and running various businesses, I came to realise that restrictions and limitations are not just imposed by governments - the biggest obstacles to achieving what we want lie behind the iron curtain that we have erected in our minds.

If you doubt this statement, try this experiment for the next week or two. Stop talking about money and how much things cost, what you would do if only you had more time, money, energy and just observe. Unless you live in an exceptional neighbourhood you will find that people talk constantly about the lack of money in their life and about limitations. You will hear people say things like:

> We can't afford it
> I knew it was too good to be true
> You can't take it with you
> If only
> You can't win
> It's okay for some
> You can't have everything you want
> What do you think I am, made of money?
> Where do you think the money is coming from?

As well as the everyday statements that we make about money, there are all those familiar old phrases that most people grew up with such as: *Money doesn't grow on trees you know; The rich get richer and the poor get poorer; money is the root of all evil and money doesn't buy you happiness.* We are constantly bombarded with messages on a daily basis that reinforce beliefs in limitations.

I was reminded recently just how wealthy we as a society really are when a taxi driver, who had come to Australia from Russia, mentioned that people on welfare in Australia live far better than 90 per cent of the entire Russian population. He went on to tell me of

Wealth tip:
When you invest your power in yourself, you will always be powerful.

31

a Russian couple who had to wait 15 years to be eligible for a one bedroom flat with a shared bathroom.

On the other hand, there are people who do not talk about how tough things are, they exude success. This group drives nice cars, wears designer labels, live in the best suburbs but behind the facades there often lies a mountain of debt and insecurity. Wealth of this sort does not bring happiness as it is based on the good opinion of others. It is precarious at best and creates unnecessary stress and tension.

It is possible to create incredible wealth from nothing even in these changing times. My father left school at the age of 14. Although he grew up in Romania, he was of German descent. His training in the real world was under the guidance of successful local merchants and businessmen. When World War II broke out, my father was conscripted into the army. At the end of the war he found himself in Austria.

Deciding not to go home, my father started a business and two years later, in 1950, he decided to come to Australia. He came to Australia on a Government-sponsored assisted passage, with the official classification of a displaced person, meaning he had no passport. He could not speak English and he had just $2 to his name.

At that time migrants had to go to work where the Government sent them, which in my father's case was to a quarry in Marulan. What set my father apart from the average man was that he knew he was not limited by his circumstances. My father would work in the quarry all week and as he did not anticipate working in a quarry all his life, he would travel to Sydney on weekends and sell smallgoods. Although on a limited income, he managed to save enough to buy a panel van and some goods to sell.

On his weekend rounds my father would talk to other migrants and they would comment that they

Wealth tip:
Luck is for people who don't believe they can have what they really want. The rich make their own luck.

32

wished they had something to read. My father saw an opportunity and wrote off to some German publishers. Before long he was importing books and magazines. This small business led to my father publishing a German newspaper which in turn became the vehicle from which he set up a number of other businesses. Demand for the German language newspaper Die Woche in Australien (*The week in Australia*) grew and my father approached the leading newsagency distributor so that he could make his publication available for sale in newsagents. Their response was, "*People don't want to buy newspapers that are not in English*".

My father has an uncanny business sense and a formidable belief in himself. He **knew** there was a market for foreign language publications so he set up his own distribution company. Many years later when I worked in my father's business for a time, we were known as the Murdochs of the ethnic press, and we distributed publications in German, Spanish, Maltese, Portuguese, Vietnamese and various other languages.

My father's efforts made him a millionaire many times over despite his humble beginnings and I am fortunate to have such a role model.

Let me state emphatically at the beginning of this book that it is easy to be rich and it is easy to be happy if you choose to be. Some of you may be thinking, *Well, it's easy for him to say, his father is a millionaire*, but I can also vouch for the fact that my father does not believe in handouts. I have experienced the same struggle and setbacks as most people. I have struggled in business. I have been retrenched. I have made some decisions that were not particularly wise and I have lost a lot of money. Nevertheless, I always knew that ultimately I would succeed because I **knew** I had choices. You have choices too. It does not matter what your circumstances are today. It does not matter how far out of reach your dreams may appear to be. It does not matter what your conditioning has been. All of these

Wealth tip:
Developing a prosperous attitude is as vital as developing positive spending and saving habits.

are obstacles that can be turned into opportunities if you choose to break free.

I teach people how to be rich but the mere pursuit of money does not automatically guarantee happiness. In fact, it's a paradox of life that the more you pursue money itself, the more it eludes you. Money is a means of exchange and the freedom and quality of life it can provide is a wonderful incentive to pursue riches. However, to create financial abundance you need to do more than just make the decision to be rich and happy. That is just the first important step. You need to be prepared to break down the iron curtain that exists within your mind. You do this by following your dream. Remember most people aren't rich, so choose to act differently from most people. Change what creates lack in your life. Then take action to embrace values, beliefs and emotions that support wealth creation and expansion.

Making the decision to be free

Everything starts with a decision and if you have made the decision that you want more from life than you have today, then you are already on the path to freedom. Now you have to reinforce that decision with action. The first place to begin is with what you *allow* into your mind. Yes, I did say *allow*, as your outer circumstances are a direct result of what you think you can have. What you thought yesterday has created your world today and what you think today creates your world tomorrow.

You have probably heard people liken the mind to a computer. In fact the mind is far more powerful than any computer man has invented. Your inner computer, or the subconscious as we know it, contains programmes on how to eat, walk, talk, heal, solve problems and protect you from danger. When you see a piece of food that you really love you may start salivating because your magnificent mind has stored in its

Ultimately we know deeply that the other side of fear is freedom.

Marilyn Ferguson

memory bank the taste and good feelings associated with that food. This wonderful computer has absolutely nothing to do with intelligence or circumstances. It works the same for everyone. Bill Gates, the founder of Microsoft and the richest man in the world, has the same internal computer working for him as you have for you. You either choose to have your magnificent mind working for you or against you.

As I am writing this, there is an article in the Sunday newspaper about Bill Gates' massive wealth which says that, assuming he worked on every business day since Microsoft was founded in 1975, for 14 hours a day, he has earned around $1.46 million per hour.

He definitely did not entertain negative beliefs despite the obstacles he had to overcome in the early days.

Regardless of how positive you are about life, you still need to deal with negative thoughts. It's all part of the balance of life. I have two techniques for dealing with negative thoughts. One technique is that I think of a negative thought as passing wind. I say to myself, *Phew, where did that thought come from? I don't want to hang around with that and then I think of something else, something positive.* Another technique is to imagine myself standing on a glass plate. Underneath the plate is running water with different coloured fish. Whenever I have a negative thought I think of it as a fish swimming past underneath me. Since I don't want to give that negative thought any energy, I just let it swim by and concentrate on something positive.

If you are serious about being rich and happy you cannot afford the indulgence of negative thinking. Some experts estimate that we have 60,000 thoughts a day and these thoughts constantly reinforce our belief system. Being positive for a short period each day is not enough if for the rest of the day we allow fear and worry thoughts to run amok.

Did you know that the average speaker can say 125 words per minute, but a listener can process 400 to 600 words a minute?

HMM... SOMETIMES I WISH MY MIND WASN'T SO FERTILE.

Talking about your money problems constantly with a friend is an indulgence that you can no longer afford.

Change your perspective

One of the most common phrases that we hear everyday is I *can't afford it*. When you make that statement, where does it take you? Nowhere, because I *can't afford it* is a statement of a belief that leads nowhere. It doesn't make you feel good or give you hope. If anything, every time you repeat that simple phrase you probably feel a little worse.

But take those same words and turn them into a question that becomes, *How can I afford it?* And you get a different perspective on the same situation. How do you feel – optimistic, expectant? Words have the power to transform your life.

When you ask yourself a question, your mind automatically looks for solutions. If you tell your mind it can't be done, it believes you and the search ends. When you ask a question, even though you may forget about the question and get on with your everyday activities, your subconscious remembers. It works much like the periscope on a submarine and is constantly on the look out for a way to get you what you want.

You can transform all of your self-limiting phrases into questions that can transform your life. Just imagine if instead of saying, I can't win, you changed it to, *How can we all win in this situation?* Or instead of saying, *You can't have everything that you want* you asked instead, *How can I have everything that I want?*

Listed below are some phrases that are a part of the language we hear every day. By being proactive, as opposed to being reactive, you have the power to transform your life.

Reactive/victim vocabulary	Proactive/responsible vocabulary
We can't afford it	How can we afford it?
I knew it was too good to be true	Let's find a way to make it last
You can't take it with you	How can I leave a legacy?
If only	I will
You can't win	How can I win?
It's okay for some	Thank you, that's for me
You can't have everything you want	How can I have everything I want?
What do you think I am, made of money?	I prefer to choose something else

Where do you think the money is coming from?	Let's see whether we really want/need this right now
I must	I prefer
I can't	I choose

As you observe yourself making reactive statements or ones which imply that you are not in charge of your life, turn them into assertive statements which indicate that you are choosing your own direction. As you do this, you will feel more and more in control of your life and that you are choosing your own destiny.

Positive thinking works because positive thinkers dwell on what they want. Always think about what you want and you will attract it into your life.

The easiest way to create new software for your magnificent computer is through your thoughts. By constantly choosing positive thoughts, thoughts of abundance and freedom, you establish new beliefs rather than those beliefs that have been thrust upon you by your childhood conditioning and the world at large. But beliefs need to be transformed into knowings before you can really live your dream to its fullest.

Sow what you wish to harvest

You can also think of your mind as a garden. Your garden will contain the plants you have planted as well as weeds which will grow by themselves. If you sow carrots you won't reap cabbages. If you want your carrots to grow nice and juicy you will have to pull out the weeds. So it is with your mind. By thinking positive thoughts you will produce positive results in your life. The negative thoughts will still be around, but it is your choice whether you give them more energy by dwelling on them or rendering them powerless by ignoring them.

It is quite simply a matter of choice, and how you decide to think is one of your most important choices.

Wayne Dyer

Results take time

When you plant carrots in your garden, it will be

some time before you can harvest them. In the same way, it takes time for you to develop new thoughts, beliefs and habits. It won't happen overnight. You need to keep reinforcing the new positive thoughts for at least 30 days before they become your new beliefs. Remember, there is a season to sow and a season to reap, but you don't do both in the same season.

Know you will succeed

A knowing is where you *allow* no doubt. As I said earlier, my father knew he would succeed - that is what made him successful. It was not the times nor the circumstances that worked in his favour, people who succeed at the highest levels *know*. Stephen Covey calls this unconscious competence. I also use the word *allow* in this context because it is a choice. It would be a rare person who never experiences a twinge of doubt. We are human after all, but the choice comes from whether you allow that doubt to exist within your consciousness. That is the one thing that we all share, no matter what the colour of our skin, our intelligence or personal circumstances are, we choose what we allow into our minds.

The biggest obstacle in our path is self delusion. There are some who convince themselves that they have to have *things* in order to feel a certain way. Take for example someone who constantly spends. Some of these people will say that they need to be surrounded by nice possessions, clothes or cars in order to feel prosperous. They are faking it until they make it. Most people have enough common sense to know that spending all of your money on consumer goods does not make you rich.

Some people dismiss the success of others as being good luck or being in the right place at the right time. Luck is destiny not personally guided. When people do not feel secure they resort to luck, but you have a far greater chance of succeeding by taking

If a person consistently concentrates on what he doesn't have he will get less and less of what he wants.

Andrew Matthews

charge of your own destiny than you do of winning the lottery.

What are your odds of winning the lottery? The odds for a first division win (that is a prize in excess of $300,000) in the lottery are less than 8 million to one. Not odds in your favour.

Thank you, that's for me

We play a little game in our family where we reinforce what we want in our lives. Whenever we see a car, a house, some clothes or other items we would love to have we say out loud, "Thank you, that's for me." This is a simple method of acknowledging what you want and is something that is easy to do whether you are a child or an adult.

Try it yourself. See how you feel after doing this for a whole day, then try it for a week. Soon you will start attracting all sorts of wonderful things into your life.

Fear and doubt are the real enemies. Not your circumstances, your intelligence, your luck, your parents, or even your partner. Taking a chance and going for what you really want in life means that you will probably confront many fears. You won't always know what is around the next corner, but in breaking free you will trade boredom for passion, security for abundance, fear for gratitude and struggle for freedom. Which road will you choose?

In Summary

1. Make the decision to be free.

2. Take charge of your thoughts.

3. Transform all beliefs into knowings by allowing no doubt.

4. Ensure you always talk positively about money and other aspects of your life. Turn negative phrases into positive possibilities by asking questions. How can I do this?

5. Play the "Thank you, that's for me" game and see how much fun you can have.

Don't cling to the past, rejecting new concepts and new challenges.

The negative mental attitude blocks the creative processes from true expression causing mental inertia, which is to live in a vacuum, to mentally wither and die on the vine.

Brian Adams

Chapter Three

How to get beyond survival

Change your attitude and your actions at the same time and you can have anything that you want.

Anne Hartley

A sandwich could be all that stands between you and your dreams.

Imagine an elite athlete going off to compete in a world competition without training or preparation. Or a doctor just out of medical school performing brain surgery. These things just don't happen because we know that to excel at anything it takes knowledge and lots of practise. Yet one of the most important subjects in life, how to make money, manage it and make it grow, is not taught in school. As a consequence, most people don't have the inner resources on which to base wise financial decisions. No wonder only two per cent achieve financial independence.

Successful people believe in themselves and their ability to make the right decisions. They still make mistakes, we all do, but they know that failure is only temporary and that even problems can be opportunities. To believe that life will be perfect once you achieve all of your goals is foolhardy - life is full of problems, which I'd rather think of as challenges. The difference however, is in knowing that you have the inner resources to turn any situation around. Very few people are born with total confidence. Most of us acquire confidence by developing attitudes and habits that support our goals.

American financial coach Rennie Gabriel met a lady who had a mentally handicapped cousin. While her cousin was employable, having an IQ in the low 80s, he could only get jobs paying the minimum wage. At a young age he was trained to pay himself the first 20 per cent of any income he earned, and after handling obligations like rent, food, etc., he could spend the rest on whatever he wanted.

Because he always paid himself first and he was mentally handicapped, he did not think of any excuses, justifications, or create a clever way to avoid doing what he was trained to do with money. Despite working low-paying jobs, by the time he was in his 30's he had saved over $100,000.[1]

Change your attitude and habits

Thinking positively is a great habit to develop but just thinking positively and ignoring the facts can lead you into a deep hole. Anne Hartley, a former financial planner and author of three books on money says, "If your habits don't support your goal then you need to change them, but just changing habits doesn't always guarantee success. Just using behaviour modification to change something is like swimming against the tide. It may work, but it's hard work. To achieve lasting success you need to change your attitude and habits at the same time". In her book *Debt Free* [2] Anne explains it this way:

I will continue to let others predict, but only I can determine what I will, can, or cannot do.

Marva Collins

What were you thinking about today? Were you wondering how you were going to pay your bills, or concerned that you may lose your job? Whatever thoughts circulate in your mind will dictate your feelings. If you are thinking 'There is not enough money to go around, how am I going to pay the mortgage or the bills?' then you're probably going to feel depressed or a failure. If you're thinking about your next holiday, or your new home, then you're likely to feel optimistic and cheerful. Our beliefs, thoughts *and feelings make up our attitude. How we **feel** makes up our attitude. Does your attitude support you or sabotage you?*

You can't think positively and feel depressed. You can't worry about money and plan to be rich. When we allow ourselves to dwell on what we don't want, we give our power away. It's tempting at times, but it is not worth the price that we have to pay. If you are in a difficult situation then the worst thing you can do is bury your head in the sand. Just hoping the problem will go away, or more accurately not talking to your creditors, not opening your mail or blaming your partner will not work. Problems don't simply go away by themselves. The best thing you can do is to ask yourself the question, *How can I turn this situation around*? The right questions can lead you to finding a solution.

Our emotions contribute enormously to how successful we are with money. Too often we let our emotions run away with us and we compensate for other problems in our lives by spending and living beyond our means. Making money is really very simple: spend less than you earn and save and invest at least 10 to 20 per cent of your income. If it is that simple, then why aren't more people doing it?

There is only one explanation why so few people fail to reach financial freedom. So few are willing to pay the price. So few are willing to cut back on their lifestyle and spend less than they earn. So few are willing to take the risks. So few are willing to set their sights high and start climbing. Most people want to become rich overnight. We have been conditioned to want immediate gratification. That is what makes us a slave to money. You can break free but you must be prepared to pay the price of self-discipline, which reminds me of two quotes by E James Rohn where he says:

Being happy can be hard work sometimes. It is like maintaining a nice home - you've got to hang on to your treasures and throw out the garbage.

Andrew Matthews.

"We must all suffer from one of two pains: the pain of discipline or the pain of regret. The difference is discipline weighs ounces while regret weighs tons."

And, "Discipline is the foundation upon which all success is built. Lack of discipline inevitably leads to failure."

Sadly, only a small number of those who read this book will actually make the commitment, even though they agree with the concept.

Everyone makes mistakes. If you knew better, you would have done things differently, but you didn't. It is possible to leave mistakes behind and start afresh. You don't do this by running away and pretending everything is rosy but by reassessing your situation. You do it by making new decisions. You do it by making different choices.

"If it wasn't for money," Sue said, "we would have a happy marriage but we fight about money all the time". Although both Sue and Peter worked and enjoyed a good income, there was never enough money to go around. Peter worked full-time and had a second job on Saturdays while Sue worked part-time five evenings a week. They have three children. As well as having a mortgage on their home and a car loan they had numerous credit card debts. All of their income went towards servicing these commitments so that whenever they wanted to buy presents, clothes, or their car needed repairs they would dip into the money that normally went towards paying off their loans. As you can imagine with this strategy it wasn't long before they were in a deep hole. You can only go on juggling credit for so long. One day it finally catches up with you.

Wealth tip:
If you are totally dependent on another person for every dollar you give your power away.

Peter lamented, "Sue is always on my back to work harder. But I'm working at full capacity now. As well as my full-time job I work every Saturday. I'm so tired I find myself yelling at the kids over nothing. Sue is always complaining and we are never at home at the same time. I sometimes wonder why I bothered getting married in the first place, we never do anything together any more."

Working harder is not the long-term solution to Sue and Peter's problems, although it may help them out of a hole temporarily. Although many people live this way it has to affect your quality of life. Peter blamed Sue for wanting too much and Sue blamed Peter for not being able to provide her with a better lifestyle. Incidentally, blame takes you nowhere. It is just wasted energy. Sue and Peter's marriage was likely to become another statistic unless they worked together on finding a solution.

Peter's solution was to sell the house, pay out all their debts and start again. Sue was dead against this idea. They compromised by doing my *Super Secrets to Riches* home-study programme (this course teaches basic money management skills) and they made a commitment to work on it together.

Before they began they agreed to a few rules. The first one was that they would not fight about money. They made a pact to be kind to each other rather than scoring points by being right. Being right may make you feel better temporarily but it doesn't change anything and it spells death to a relationship. They also decided that they would set aside a specific time each week to work on their financial plan and that they would have these discussions somewhere outside of their home, because that is where they always fought about money in the past. As Sunday was the only day they spent together, they decided to take the children on a picnic each week and while the children played, they set to work on the exercises in the course and began formulating their first ever financial plan.

One of the biggest mistakes that most people make is that they fail to plan. They may initially use discipline to save a deposit for a home but once they have achieved that goal all other planning goes out the window. Hence the reason for Sue and Peter's problems – they didn't have any plans or goals, they just spent. Sue and Peter's main obstacle was consumer

The single most powerful asset we all have is our mind. If it is trained well, it can create enormous wealth in what seems to be an instant.

Robert Kiyosaki

debt, and consumer debt is one of the major problems that our society faces today. Consumer debt can send you broke, break up relationships and create as much havoc as a major life crisis.

Taking responsibility

From their weekly discussions Sue and Peter each chose tasks that they would work on during the week. Peter decided to check out banks which offered the best deals on cheque accounts and credit cards. He also decided to do some research on home loans at the same time. Sue chose to look for ways to reduce their household spending without reducing their lifestyle.

The end result was that Sue was able to cut their spending $100 a week by learning how to shop better. Peter discovered that by refinancing all of their debts onto their mortgage they could actually save $1,000 a month in repayments. This allowed him to give up his second job and still be substantially better off.

Let me caution you at this point that this solution is not for everyone. Naturally if you don't own a home it is not an option. On the other hand, you may not have sufficient equity in your home. You may also be unable to do this because of a poor credit rating. Or you may be unable to borrow enough because you are already overcommitted. Just as there are many challenges, there are also different solutions.

Many great financial problems are caused by going along with the crowd and trying to keep up with the Joneses.

Robert Kiyosaki

The other consideration is the cost. If Sue and Peter just continued paying the minimum payment on their mortgage, their consumer debts would actually cost them more. Although they are paying a lower interest rate, they are spreading their repayments over a much longer period. However, Sue and Peter plan to pay more on their mortgage so that this debt is cleared in record time. This is a good strategy. But don't consider this option unless you are absolutely sure you can trust yourself to stick to your plan.

One couple I know consolidated their debts and refinanced their mortgage in a home equity loan. They thought they were being smart. However, because the type of loan they had was one where they could continually draw up to their credit limit, they never paid anything off. There was always something to spend their money on. At first they thought it was time for them to take an overseas holiday. Then they wanted a new car. They also paid one per cent more in interest to have this facility. Eventually, as they approached retirement, they still owed $50,000 on their mortgage, which was more than they had borrowed when they first bought their home. They had to move to a cheaper area in order to be able to survive on a pension. Refinancing works if you do not continue spending. It is disastrous if you do not change your patterns.

Reducing your spending does not have to mean reducing your lifestyle. The reason most people resist the idea of making a budget is because they mistakenly believe that budgets mean deprivation, in fact just the opposite is the case. A budget is just a spending plan that allows you to make choices that helps you to achieve your larger goals. Commonsense tells us that if we spend everything today, we are not going to have anything left over for the bigger things in life.

The object of this book is to give you freedom, not to hamper your lifestyle by placing restrictions upon it, but that does not mean you do not have to make choices. If throwing money away and living beyond your means makes you happy then do it. But be sure it really makes you happy. The problem with quick fixes is that they offer temporary highs. When you go shopping and buy something you like, you feel good for a short while but you will be lucky if the feeling lasts a week. Before long you become accustomed to having that new possession in your life and it doesn't bring the gratification, or the attention it did when it was new, so you go in search of another fix.

It is in your moments of decision that your destiny is shaped.

Anthony Robbins

49

The question you have to answer is, *What makes you happy?* Most of us would opt for a life of comfort where money is not restricted. Imagine taking holidays whenever you want, living in nice surroundings, having money to buy those you love presents, or even to go out to dinner on a regular basis without feeling guilty or asking yourself if you can afford it. All this can be yours when you plan to be rich and sometimes that means giving up instant gratification in favour of the bigger plan. However, as I said before, changing the way you spend does not necessarily mean doing without. It means learning to achieve the same results by being smarter with your money.

By ceasing blame and taking responsibility for changing their situation Sue and Peter were able to work out a plan that provided more money for their bigger goals and also gave them more time together. Where there is a will, there is always a solution.

Budgeting is about self-discipline

To some people the idea of self-discipline implies restriction. I prefer to look at discipline another way.

In the Bible, a disciple was a follower. A person who followed Christ's teachings and who taught others. Whenever I think of self-discipline, I think of myself as a follower and teacher of the choices I make. By choosing to budget, I am following a behaviour pattern which has provided the basis for financial freedom. As a result of the sacrifices I made years ago, I am now able to go on holidays and come back to a bigger bank balance than before I left because my investments have been generating an income while I have been at play. These same investments have allowed me to send my children overseas to go to school, learn new languages and to enjoy new experiences. They have allowed us to help others and to provide a temporary home for overseas exchange students. They have allowed us to travel and to enjoy a comfortable lifestyle.

Wealth tip:
A good budget should allow for some luxuries and fun.

50

It did require sacrifices and choices and still does. At times it has been quite tough. This disciple was following a teaching, with a vision in mind. It was that vision, that belief in a life of financial freedom that made the temporary sacrifice worthwhile. Become a disciple, a believer in your own ability to create financial freedom and you will find the path of financial self-discipline easier to follow.

Be a smart consumer

A smart consumer is someone who buys intelligently and shops within an assigned budget. A budget keeps a wise money manager from being derailed from his financial goal. A budget eases the decision making process of how to spend your money. Like a road map, it lays out in advance how you choose to spend your money.

How do you make a concerted effort to buy only what you need and really want and ignore the enormous pressures to buy what you don't need and don't really want? How do you stick to your budget?

Start by understanding the difference between planned shopping and impulse buying. A smart consumer plans their spending and shops wisely. Before shopping, they do their research and plan what they want to buy. In other words, they do their homework first, before they even walk into a store and then apply a healthy dose of self-discipline when they are there.

My wife and I have a system for shopping that we call our **MESS** programme.

M stands for "make a list". Making a shopping list is vital because it forces you to decide ahead of time what you really need. To make up a list, you also need to check first what you already have. You need to do a stocktake or take measurements before you leave the house.

When the will comes into conflict with the imagination, the imagination always carries the day.

Emile Coue

E is for "evaluate". What are the basic necessities for your household. My wife makes three separate lists for toiletries, pantry and the house. Then she identifies them in each of the those categories.

S is for "shop the ads". You can treat this as the most exciting part of the shopping game. If you look upon it as an intellectual challenge to hunt for the lowest prices and to sniff out the best value deals, you can have a lot of fun with this.

S is for "stick to your list". My wife is great at sticking to her list but whenever I go food shopping I always buy what I like to eat or something new I would like to try out regardless of what is on the list. Either I come home with a lot more than is on the list or just some of what is on the list, or what I consider to be necessities. Needless to say this sends the budget out the window and I am in trouble! Then I include a bunch of flowers on the shopping list - as a necessity.

Often people say to me, "If the money is in my wallet, it goes. I just find a way to spend it."

That is an easy challenge to fix. These days it is not intelligent to carry large sums of money around, so if ready cash creates a temptation for you don't carry it, keep your money in the bank in an account that is not readily accessible, such as a passbook savings account. Leave your credit cards at home.

Having said that I always carry at least $100 and I suggest that once you master your finances you do this too. Firstly, you will feel more prosperous. Secondly, you will become accustomed to having money. Thirdly, you will learn to trust yourself with money.

An average salary earner will earn over one million during their working life. What will they have to show for it?

Is a sandwich a day sending you broke?

As Sue looked for ways to reduce her household spending she became aware that a large amount of their money went on lunches and take-away food. Sue was tired most mornings having worked until 11 p.m. each week night, so it was easier to give the children money to buy their lunches from the school canteen rather than make it. Now $2.50 per child for a sandwich and drink may not seem like much on a daily basis but over time it all adds up. The cost of lunch for three children, five days a week, amounted to $37.50 a week. Peter also spent around $5 each day on lunch and morning tea from the sandwich shop near his office. The total cost of lunches each week was $62.50. As Peter learnt more about his financial options he realised this money could be paying off an investment property for them, an alternative that would give them more choices and a better quality of life later on. They decided the short-term convenience was not worth the long-term consequences.

Another pattern they had fallen into was buying takeaways. This luxury cost them at least $30 each week. As a result of making choices and recognising the opportunities that lay before them they were able to reduce their spending in this area by $92.50 a week. Sue estimated that the cost of preparing lunches and an extra dinner would be less than $20 a week, so they were able to conservatively save around $70 a week in this one area alone.

By the way, Sue and Peter still don't cook on weekends now. Sue just cooks two meals in one. Sue said, "When I am making dishes such as spaghetti bolognaise or a curry, it is just as easy to cook double the volume and freeze one portion. That way, I still don't have to cook on weekends and we don't have the extra cost associated with takeaway. We just pop whatever is in the freezer in the microwave. What I have learnt about money is that planning makes a big difference. A little forethought has saved us thousands of dollars and probably our marriage as well".

The good life costs a lot and there is an alternative, but poverty isn't very appealing.

It is not uncommon for the average family to literally throw away $100 a week. That $100 invested wisely is what can make you rich. If you estimate the total amount that Sue and Peter spent on lunches over an average period of 13 years while the children were at school, you would find that canteen lunches would have cost around $19,500 and Peter's lunches, for that same time frame, would have cost $18,720. A few dollars a day may not seem like much at the time but they add up.

If Sue and Peter had invested this $70 a week, this is what they would have to show for it.

$70 a week invested at 10 per cent over 10 years
$ 62,134

$70 a week invested at 10 per cent over 20 years
$230,336

$70 a week invested at 10 per cent over 30 years
$685,671

Wealth tip:
Ask yourself: Is a sandwich a day sending you broke?

$70 a week invested at 10 per cent over 40 years
$1,918,280

Don't ever underestimate the power of saving no matter how small an amount you start with.

Compound interest can turn even small amounts into big sums that will in turn provide you with a very comfortable lifestyle that is free from money worries.

I am fortunate that my wife and I share the same financial goals. Although she chooses to work, she also takes the time to prepare most of our meals from scratch. Rather than buying ready made sauces and meals, Colette prepares them in advance from fresh ingredients. We all appreciate the extra work she goes to and feel that we eat better for it. In turn, we all share in the other household chores to support her.

As a result, our children have all learnt how to cook and look after themselves. Colette gets a break from cooking when the children prepare the meals for the family.

The money we save in this one area allows us to enjoy other activities.

Plan ahead

Sue and Peter were excited about their success and were eager to move on to the next phase and that is planning ahead. When you are in the survival phase you rarely make plans because there is simply no money left over to do anything with. However, Sue and Peter were starting to visualise a life where they had choices. A life where they wouldn't have to worry about how to pay the bills when they came in, and being able to calculate what their real cost of living was. I say real because most people kid themselves by leaving out half of the expenses that we all face, such as new tyres for the car, children's after school activities, uniforms, the dentist's bill or the cost of an unexpected illness. A realistic budget includes allowances for insurances, telephone, electricity, presents, holidays, entertainment, medical and the unexpected . They allocated a set amount each pay to a special account to cover these expenses. From a very young age, I can remember my father dividing his money between different

Wealth tip:
Revise your budget once a year, or whenever your financial situation changes.

accounts. My father never had to worry about how to pay a bill, he always planned ahead. It takes the stress out of paying bills.

In the past, Sue was responsible for paying most of the bills and she had hated doing it because there had never been enough money to go around. She gladly handed this job over to Peter who decided to pay most bills, where possible, on his credit card. Now that their spending was under control, he simply transferred money from his mortgage offset account each month to clear the credit card balance. This strategy works only if you have your spending under control. If you can't handle credit cards it would be better to use a bank account solely for this purpose.

It didn't take long before Sue and Peter were able to start their savings plan and their first goal was to ensure that three months living expenses were set aside before they set to work on their larger goals. They chose to place this money into their mortgage offset account to minimise the amount of interest payable on their home loan. A mortgage offset account does not pay interest, instead the interest component is deducted from your mortgage. Keeping spare money in this account can significantly reduce the term of your mortgage, it is easily accessible and because you don't actually earn interest you don't pay tax on it.

The secret is to spend what you have left after saving, instead of saving what you have left after spending.

Frank & Muriel Newman

If your mortgage provides a redraw facility and you don't have a spending problem, it is even better to use a line of credit facility than a mortgage offset account. You can reduce your outstanding mortgage balance by depositing your wages and savings directly into a line of credit account. This way you will pay less interest and reduce the term of your loan dramatically. The interest you pay on your home mortgage is also not tax deductible so you want to eliminate this as quickly as possible. By reducing your mortgage as quickly as possible you can use your equity to build an investment portfolio.

A line of credit facility is a powerful financing facility with major benefits. The interest on such a facility is usually higher than on a regular home loan account (because of its flexibility) and you can always redraw up to your limit when the need arises. It is great if you manage your money well. If you don't, or when interest rates are rising, it can be a nightmare. Make sure you fully understand how this facility works and keep a tight rein on your spending if you use a line of credit facility.

Within a very short period of time Sue and Peter were able to totally transform their financial situation. As they took responsibility and ceased blaming each other, they were able to find workable solutions. Most people stop there, but if you really want to be rich and happy then you need to look further to avoid petty situations becoming a problem in the future.

Victim mentality

Many nice, responsible people go through life with a victim mentality, and that is when they give their power away to others because they worry about what other people might think. I have covered this in more depth in the next chapter but I wanted to touch on an aspect of it now because it particularly relates to Sue and Peter's situation.

A common situation where many take on the role of the victim relates to sharing the bill when you eat out with others. Sue and Peter like to dine out with friends when they have funds available. Because they are on a tight budget they usually order the cheapest dishes on the menu whilst their friends who are much better off financially, order whatever they like, usually three courses, wine and liqueurs. When the time came, they usually just split the bill. For years this had been a source of resentment for both Sue and Peter but they never said anything for fear of looking cheap.

Wealthy people invest, poor people consume.

Frank & Muriel Newman

I suggested that they simply pick up the bill when it

57

arrives, calculate their share and put the money down and say, "Our share is $30" and leave it at that. If the friends argue the point, which I very much doubt they will, they should simply state that they don't drink and their share of the bill was less. Most friends will be happy to accept a fair split and often this type of situation arises out of thoughtlessness. This is an example of how you can value yourself and your money.

There are many situations where we become victims. For example, when we buy presents that cost more than we would like to pay, it is usually because we want others to think well of us.

Sue had been working evenings since the children were young, stacking shelves in a supermarket. It was hard work and it paid poorly. Usually she just gritted her teeth and got on with it because Sue believed that she had very few choices if she wanted to stay at home and be a full-time mum. Seeing the changes that taking responsibility had done for their lives, Sue changed her mindset about her work situation as well. When you do that, you often recognise opportunities that are right in front of you.

Sue loved craft work and one of the things she did was paint T-shirts. She was often asked to make them for friends and if she had the time she would do them for free. She decided to turn this hobby into a business and one of the best ways to make money is from hobbies. Sue canvassed amongst her friends and received orders but there weren't enough for her to give up her job. The next thing she did was to call in at a few local shops. She also paid $15 to participate in a car boot sale that the children's school organised as a fund raising venture. That day she sold all her stock and took orders for more. Within three months Sue was able to give up her evening job and within six months she was making $200 a week more than she did in her former job and she was doing what she loved.

Recognition of your worth will come from others once you give it to yourself.

Anne Hartley

58

Peter gave up his Saturday job and started doing tennis coaching on Saturday mornings, something that he also loved doing. Peter was able to make the same amount from his small coaching business as he had previously made from working all day Saturday.

Change your attitude and your habits and miracles will become an everyday experience.

In Summary

1. Change your attitude and habits at the same time.

2. Take responsibility for where you are today. It is the only way to make permanent change.

3. Notice where your money goes and become a smart consumer.

4. Save regularly and become a disciple. Believe in financial freedom.

5. Plan ahead.

*The greatest pleasure in life is doing
what people say you cannot do.*

Walter Bagehot

Chapter Four

Taking charge of your life

Keep away from people who try to belittle your ambition.
Small people always do that, but the really great make you
feel that you, too, can become great.

Mark Twain

**You will never be rich or completely happy until
you free yourself from the good opinion of others.**

The greatest handicap we all face is that we make
choices and decisions based on what other people
may think. In other words, we give our power away to
others. A number of years ago I came across an article
in a management magazine and unfortunately I don't
know who wrote it but it illustrates my point.

There was a man who lived by the side of a road. He
sold hot dogs. Because he was hard of hearing he had
no radio. Because his vision was poor he read no
newspapers. However, he sold good hot dogs.

As business grew he put a neon sign on the highway, advertising his hot dogs and people bought. He
increased his meat and roll orders and bought a bigger
stove. Business was doing well. Then his son came
home from university to help him.

His son told him what was happening in the world.
"Times are tough" he said, "there may be a depression

coming. You had better prepare for business to drop".

The father, who was not an educated man, thought that his son, with his university education, must know best so the father cut down his meat and roll orders. He turned off his sign to save electricity. He no longer stood on the side of the highway to sell his hot dogs and guess what? His hot dog orders fell almost overnight.

"You were right," the father said to his son, "we certainly are headed for a depression."

Some of us live our lives by accident, others by design. Too often our choices are influenced by well-meaning others. The consequence is that some of those choices can leave us feeling sad, unhappy and stuck.

A woman said to me recently, "It doesn't matter what I do, I always seem to make the wrong decision." We have all made poor choices at some stage in our lives. It's all a part of the learning process, but the only way to learn from mistakes is to move on. Avoiding making decisions in the future, for fear of making more mistakes, will only take you backwards. Nothing stands still. Economies have to grow and so do people. If you are not moving forward you are probably sliding backwards. For instance, if you save to buy your home and never save another cent, then you are going backwards. By the time you retire, you will be dependent on the old age pension and that is certainly less than the average wage. Do you want to spend your leisure years struggling just to survive? If you obtain a secure job and then never do another thing to increase your knowledge or gain additional work skills, then chances are that one day you will be made obsolete. Technology is advancing at a rapid pace and people who can't keep their skills up-to-date will be left behind. If you leave school and then gain no additional skills that can be used in the work force you will most likely end up living on the dole.

Wealth tip:
You don't need to be smart, educated or talented to be rich.

Knowledge is a powerful tool

Knowledge plus action is power. The world is full of intelligent people who aren't rich. They have lots of knowledge but don't always take the risks to put their knowledge to work.

No-one can guarantee that every decision will be the right one, but the more knowledge you have the more confidence you will develop in making the right choices. In the introduction I mentioned my experience selling investment real estate. It is sad but true that there will always be people in every industry who have so little faith in their own ability to make money honestly that they resort to deception. A few years back there was a scam involving commodity traders, in a few more years it will be something else. But a few bad apples don't spoil a crop. Don't ignore a perfectly good opportunity just because a few have to resort to this tactic.

Knowledge gives you the power to discern between a genuine opportunity and one with no merit. Until our education system changes, self-education is an essential part of gaining the required knowledge.

I once heard a man say, "Anyone who pays hundreds of dollars for a course must have rocks in his head". Well, I am one of those people who have paid thousands over the years on courses, books and tapes, and none of it has been wasted. Not all courses lived up to my expectations but I have found that if you approach everything with an open mind then you only have to get one thing from a seminar or course and it could make you ten times more than you paid for it. One woman told me of a seminar she attended many years ago that led her to start a very successful business. She said, 'I was at a seminar being presented by Denis Waitley. I think the day cost about $200. It was a long time ago, and I had never paid that sort of money before and I was a little apprehensive. That day at

Formal education will make you a living. Self education will make you a fortune.

Jim Rohn

lunch, I met a man who said he needed a service that I knew I could provide. That man became my first client and I used the principles I learnt that day to build up the business which I later sold at a considerable profit".

Incidentally, that man who doesn't believe in self-education is still in the same financial situation today that he was in 10 years ago.

Who can you trust?

One of the questions I am most commonly asked is, *How do you know who to trust?*

Firstly, I would be wary if the person giving advice has a barrow to push. By that I mean; will they personally benefit from you taking their advice? A good example is the increasing number of free or very low cost ($20 per person) seminars on negative gearing or on buying investment properties. These are usually put on by companies selling investment properties as I mentioned in the introduction. Their purpose in putting on these seminars is not to teach you the benefits of negative gearing. (It would be commercially impossible to do so for $20 a head anyway.) They are out to sell you a property. And usually buying a property of this type is not in your best interest. It is in the company's and the salesperson's best interest. But that is not to say that you won't learn anything by attending. Just be aware that there will be a sales pitch and it is not necessarily in your best interest. You need to do your own research before you invest.

You can have everything in life that you want if you'll just help enough other people to get what they want.

Zig Ziglar

I heard of a man who attended one of these seminars and bought a room in a motel. This motel had previously been operated as an independent business but the owners were selling off all the rooms and were planning to stay on as managers for a fee. That in itself should make you suspicious. If the business was that good why would they sell it and then continue to work in it?

The first 12 months saw a reasonable return on this man's investment of $80,000. After that, the room was rarely let, or so they said, as he never had access to the records. Despite low occupancy rates he still had to pay a management fee each month as well as electricity, rates, insurance etc. The property was costing this man $800 a month and he couldn't afford it. He tried to sell the property but no-one was interested and based on the return he was getting it was not a good investment. This man found that he had to continue paying a mortgage on what was virtually a white elephant or go bankrupt.

Seminars that are presented for educational purposes are my preferred option. However, don't just take all of these at face value. Think about what you are being taught. Look at the track record of the person presenting the seminar and the quality of the information supplied. How good is their understanding of the subject matter? Does the presenter walk their talk? Does the advice work for them?

All that glistens is not gold

Don't be taken in by appearances. When I did sales training we were told to have a gold case for our business cards, to wear a gold watch, look prosperous and were encouraged to drive expensive cars. All of these possessions were supposed to convey prosperity to our clients. My experience though has been that people who are genuinely wealthy don't need to be flashy about it. My personal preference is not to do business with anyone who looks like this. I am wary that most of their knowledge comes from sales training and is not direct knowledge gained through personal experience.

How many people do you know who are living beyond their means in order to impress others? Some may deny that this is the case, I *am doing it for me* they claim, but rarely is this the case. What other people

Wealth tip:
Life is like a boomerang, what you give out you get back.

will think of you is one of the strongest forms of bondage that keeps you imprisoned by your own choice.

I also take note of how people treat others. Some men treat women badly. This could be their wife, girl-friend or someone at work. If they treat others that way they will be the same with you one day. I won't do business with people whose values conflict with mine. That is not to say that everyone's values have to be the same as mine but there is a difference between having different beliefs and values and having conflicting beliefs and values.

Become a rhinoceros

Rhinoceros Success[3] was written by Scott Alexander and it is a very humorous account that likens success to developing the traits of a rhinoceros. Scott says, "Rhinoceroses charge with singleness of purpose." Think about it. Can you imagine the full force of a rhinoceros in pursuit of his prey being suddenly distracted and undecided. His indecision would cause him to lose speed, direction and while he was thinking about it, his prey would escape and he would go hungry. That is what humans do every day.

You need to be single minded about what you want and allow no doubt. That often means keeping your goals to yourself. Most people don't set out to sabotage us deliberately but that is often what they do, and we do it to others when we tell them that they cannot have what they want. Sometimes we don't always utter our words of doubt but we can convey our feelings with just a look or a gesture. One man said to me that every time he shared a new idea with his wife, she would turn away slightly from him. He knew that without her saying a word, she thought he was only dreaming. That one gesture was usually enough to dampen his enthusiasm and he would give up on the idea. Please don't let anyone steal your dreams. Dreams are important.

Every time you talk about what you want to people who are not part of helping you achieve it, you sow seeds of doubt. But that's just what they are: seeds. The more you talk about what you want the more fertiliser and water you give these seeds and the doubts soon become young seedlings. Before you know it your garden of dreams is full of fully grown weeds. As any gardener knows keeping the weeds at bay is a full-time job.

You avoid doubts taking hold by not spreading the weed seeds in the first place, so unless it is absolutely necessary, don't talk about what you plan to do. You may want to talk to a professional adviser, or to a teacher, even toss ideas around with someone close to you and that's okay. Just choose who you share your dreams with carefully. The masses don't think big and will only tell you their reality. There will even be "experts" that tell you it can't be done. It's your choice whether you listen to them or show them that it can be done. Remember what others believe does not have to be your reality. If in doubt tell no-one.

That is why Henry David Thoreau said, "If one advances confidently in the direction of his own dreams and endeavours to lead the life in which he has

Wealth tip:
If you persist at anything you are passionate about you will eventually succeed.

imagined he will meet with a success unexpected in common hours."

There is a certain type of bamboo that takes years and years for the roots to grow underground before any shoots appear on the surface. Then one day a stalk pops up and in no time it is a flourishing plant. If you kept digging it up to see how it was going, you would destroy the root system and eventually kill the plant. Sometimes you just have to trust when the going seems slow that you are building a strong foundation and ultimately you will reap the rewards.

Clarence Smithison said that, "faith is the ability to see the invisible - to believe the incredible. That is what enables you to receive what the masses think is impossible."

Be persistent

If you really, really, really, want something then you can have it but often, most times in fact, you have to be persistent. Colonel Sanders received 1009 rejections before someone finally agreed to use his idea. The result was Kentucky Fried Chicken. On retirement all that Colonel Sanders owned was a little restaurant that was broke because the main highway had been diverted elsewhere. His customers had been telling him for years how great his chicken was so he had the idea of selling his recipe to other restaurant owners in return for a small share of the takings. I don't imagine that it would be easy at any age to be laughed at but being at retirement age would have to make it a little harder to take. That is what happened to Colonel Sanders. He was laughed at and told **'No'** 1009 times. The fact that he kept count demonstrates the influence this had on him. But did he give up? Well you know the answer to that one. Despite continued rejections he didn't give up. He travelled around the country, sleeping in his car until he found someone who said yes. The rest is history.

Some men see things that are, and ask why? I see things that are not yet, and ask why not?

Robert F Kennedy

Lack of persistence and the belief that they cannot really have what they want is what prevents most people from changing. Remember you are in charge of your life. If you want something badly enough there is a way.

Most people are quitters. This is wonderful news for those of us who decide to be successful. For us, it means that if we stick to what we are doing, we will, in a short time, be ahead of the masses. As the saying goes, "A big shot is simply a little shot that kept shooting!".

Be alert

Rhinoceroses are also alert. In the jungle you would soon die of starvation if you were not alert and on the lookout. Opportunities are all around you but if you spend all your time dwelling on the past or living in the future you will not recognise them. Have you ever decided that you would like to buy a certain type of car and suddenly everywhere you look, on the road, in the newspaper, on TV you see just the car that you want. When you focus on anything, your subconscious alerts you to the opportunities around you. It's not that these things were not there in the past, it is just that until you were interested, you never really noticed them. It is the same with opportunities. You don't notice them until you focus on what you want.

There is a big difference between being alert and being conned. Chances are that those who chase get-rich-quick schemes usually get poor even quicker. If in doubt seek advice from an expert, but remember the choice is yours.

I recently spoke to a man who was interested in buying my *Super Secrets to Wealth do-it-yourself Real Estate Investment Home Study Course*. When it came to making payment I offered him our credit card payment option. He explained that he did not have a credit card any more. He said he was busily paying off his previous

Most fears never amount to anything.

debts and had cut up his credit cards. He wanted to learn about my contrary approach to investing in real estate because he had lost tens of thousands of dollars on two get-rich-quick schemes. Both of these deals offered spectacular returns, the only problem was that they collapsed before he could get his capital back, let alone any profits.

Maintain balance

Achieving goals can be a lot of fun but be wary of being so caught up in what the future holds that you forget about enjoying today. Ken Blanchard heard this quote in Japan, "Managing for profit or the bottom line only is like playing tennis with your eye on the scoreboard and not on the ball." Always looking to the future can mean that you miss opportunities today, not to mention the fact that many of life's greatest pleasures come from everyday events.

Develop single-minded focus, know where you are going, take charge of your life and enjoy each day. Always take time to smell the roses and marvel at life's miracles and the miracle of life itself. Take time out to go for a walk along the beach, go into the bush and just stop to look, smell and listen. Realise what a marvellous and fascinating world we live in. Think about the incredible intelligence that is part of creation. How can a tiny seed grow into a massive tree? How can a tiny fertilised ovum grow into a perfect human being? We are surrounded by miracles every day. Take time out to meditate and to give thanks to our creator.

Albert Einstein once said: "There are only two ways to live your life. One is as though nothing is a miracle. The other is as though everything is a miracle."

Wealth tip:
Give thanks daily for what you have and what you expect to have.

In Summary

1. You are in charge of your life.

2. Knowledge can lead to power if you take action.

3. Take care who you take advice from.

4. Don't be fooled by appearances.

5. Learn to focus on what you want.

6. Be persistent.

7. Be alert for opportunities.

8. Maintain balance and give thanks.

Decide what you want,
decide what you are willing to
exchange for it.
Establish your priorities
and go to work.

HL Hunt

Chapter Five

Mastering your income

Planning may not guarantee success but statistics prove that unless you make some plan you are guaranteed to fail.

The key to success in business or personal finances is planning.

Lottery winners are notorious for throwing away their winnings. Unless you look after your money it will slip through your fingers. Success doesn't just happen – it takes planning and that usually means making choices. No-one else can tell you what those choices should be, we can only make suggestions. For instance if you work all week and a have a busy family life you may decide that it is better for your happiness and peace of mind to have a cleaner, even though it does cost more than doing it yourself. On the other hand, you may decide that the area in which you can save money is by reducing takeaway meals. Australians spend millions each day on takeaway food and one small luxury could be all that is standing between you and your dreams.

Some of you may be thinking, *but I want to be rich so I won't have to scrimp and save*, and that is a very valid reason. Even if you become rich overnight, you still need to look after your money and make choices. That is what this chapter is all about. Making choices as to what to do with your money. The odds of winning money are pretty slim, so if you are really serious about being rich, then it is best to start where you are.

Begin with a budget

I don't like budgets, but I highly value financial freedom. Before you can rearrange your personal finances you need to know where your money goes. Think of your personal finances as you would a business. If I was called in to give advice on a business, one of the first things that I would look at would be their profit and loss statement. A profit and loss statement shows the income and expenditure of any business. Your budget is your profit and loss statement. You need to know how much comes in and how much goes out so that you can make choices that support the life you want to live.

Once you have worked out your figures, you need to find a way to save at least 10 per cent of your income. If you already have disposable income, that is great. Just remember those incidentals. If you are really smart, you may be able to save more than 10 per cent and I'll tell you why as we go along.

The power of saving

Robert Kiyosaki, author and teacher on making money, gives the example of how to make your child a billionaire [4]. It is really very simple. Just save $100 a month from the day your child is born. Place this money into an investment that pays 16 per cent per annum, for 74 years and it would amount to a billion dollars. Mind boggling isn't it?

There are two things that you might question in this strategy. One is that 16 per cent is a very high return. It is, but it is not impossible to achieve when you know how. The other aspect is the time factor. You and I probably won't be around when our children turn 74 and who wants to wait that long? Well naturally no-

A survey was conducted in the US to find out the major difference between millionaires and billionaires. They discovered that millionaires read their goals once a day while billionaires read their goals twice a day. It was as simple as that!

Paul Hanna

74

one does but that doesn't mean those assets can't be enjoyed a lot sooner. Even while your children are enjoying them they can still be growing in value. The message I want to convey in this book is that it is easier to have your money working for you, than you working for it.

One of the rules I live by is to divert a portion of my income (at least 10 per cent) into income-producing assets. I then use the income from these assets to pay for my luxuries.

Most people who stay poor use their income to pay for their luxuries. That way they never get to have investments which will significantly increase their income in future years.

Having said that, I also think it is vitally important to live your life in the present. One of my favourite authors and mentors is Dr Wayne Dyer. He has helped me to understand that the only time that really matters is right now. Your power is in the present moment. The past is over and you can't change it anyway. What is done is done! The future hasn't happened yet and there is no point spending energy on what may or may not happen. The point of power is in the present. The choices you make right now will shape your destiny. You can design your life the way you want it - starting right now.

Plan for the future, but live your life in the present.

An article appeared in a US *Money Magazine* in 1996 about a woman called Anne Scheiver. Anne lost all her money in the great depression when her brother invested her life savings. Ten years later, in 1944, she managed to save enough to start investing again, only this time she did it herself, starting with $5,000. By the time she died in 1995 she had personally built up her fortune to the incredible sum of $20 million. That's all it took on an average wage, just 50 years to make $20

Wealth tip:
You cannot succeed unless you are prepared to fail.

million! Just think of the incredible fortune Bill Gates has amassed in just 23 years to become the richest man in the world.

Not everyone wants to be a billionaire or even a millionaire, nor does everyone want to be an investment whiz. You don't have to be. Your goal may be to live a comfortable life. Whatever it is, the means are within your reach by doing a little planning. The first place to start is by looking at how much you spend, where you spend it, and look for ways to save and invest.

How much can you save?

One family that I know bought at least three takeaway meals a week because of lack of time. The mother said to me, "It's not that we even like the food particularly but it is convenient." She hated cooking but a health crisis made her reassess their eating habits and she began looking for ways to create meals that were nutritious and most importantly, easy to prepare. She rediscovered a passion for cooking that she hadn't experienced since the early days of her marriage. She said, "I think what I hated the most was that after a long day at work we would all come home and everyone else would relax in front of the TV while I was stuck in the kitchen cooking by myself. You can't help but feel resentful when you never get any time off. This time though, I knew we had to change. I discovered cooking Thai and Indian food was easy to prepare and it tasted so good, no-one ever wants takeaways now. I now look on cooking as my hobby and my family love it. Everyone helps out and we are saving money as well."

Some people may say that I am tight because I save paperclips, recycle envelopes, re-use postage stamps, pick up aluminium cans for my kids and I always bend down to pick up money I find on the street, even five cents. The throwaway habits our society has been

Wealth tip:
The rich don't use credit for consumer items.

accustomed to, not only cost you money, they are harmful for our environment. Being tight with money has enabled us to own a number of properties and have an asset base in excess of a million dollars and my family and I have also travelled extensively overseas. In a few weeks my wife and I are travelling to Canada for three weeks to do a retreat-style course that we both are looking forward to. Being careful about the little things has allowed us to enjoy a more affluent lifestyle.

Don't misunderstand and think that I am encouraging you to be miserly. I am not. I heard of a successful businessman whose family were living below the poverty line. One day his family left him and all he had left was his money. Being careful is about making choices so that you can have a better quality of life rather than throwing money away on items that are really not important to you, which is what most people do. Most people aren't aware just how powerful saving and investing can be and how it can transform your life.

60 ways to save money

I have listed below 60 ways to save money. See if you can add to this list and if you can, please let me know so that I can share your ideas with others.

1. Take your lunch to work

2. Prepare lunches for children at school

3. Reduce the number of takeaway meals

4. Eliminate frozen food from your shopping and freeze your own

5. Shop no more than once a week

6. You'll save even more on food by shopping fortnightly or monthly if you have storage space

7. Only food shop after you have eaten (you buy more when you are hungry)

8. Stay away from the shops when you are depressed

9. Check out the top shelves in the supermarket, they often house the cheaper products

10. Generic brands can save you up to 40 per cent

11. Shop the walls in your supermarket. All the staples are around the walls, the aisles contain the luxuries

12. Swap traditional cleansers for natural products for cleaning such as bi-carb soda and vinegar and you'll save. You will also be helping the environment

13. Shop at the end of a day or Sunday after 4 p.m. Perishables are marked down substantially at this time

14. Join a co-op or start your own and buy direct from the produce markets

15. Shop for clothes only twice a year, once for summer and once for winter

16. Shop when it is genuine sale time

17. Shop at the end of the season

18. Buy clothes that don't need dry cleaning

19. Shop for presents during sale time

20. Buy direct from factory outlets or seconds shops

21. Invest in magazines that tell you where to shop and save

22. Ask if there is a discount for cash, in fact, always ask for a discount no matter what! It embarrasses your children no end!

23 Play one retailer against another and ask for a better price

24. Use the local library and only buy books that you want to keep

25. Plan your gift spending, better still, make your own gifts

26. Make gift cards instead of buying them. Get the kids to help. Recycle last year's Christmas cards and save the trees

27. Join a babysitting club

28. Join a local barter club

29. Save on car airconditioning by buying a light coloured car, dark cars absorb more heat

30. Use your car airconditioning only to cool the vehicle then turn it off, don't use it all year round

31. Save on household heating costs by learning how to use natural resources, even the colour of your house can reduce or increase the cost of heating

32. Drawing the blinds early in winter stops the heat from the sun escaping

33. Protect your house from the sun in summer by planting deciduous trees

34. Re-use and recycle as much as you can. You save money as well as helping the environment

35. When building or extending, consider where you place your hot water system. The closer it is to kitchen and bathroom the more you will save on hot water bills

36. Consider energy saving appliances when replacing whitegoods

37. Consider buying your car at the end of a month, this is the closing period for sales and if a salesperson needs to boost his figures it's the time you'll get the biggest discount

38. Buy a car from a government auction

39. Be wary of buying at just any auction. Set your price before bidding starts and make sure you have researched the retail price first

40. Choose a credit card with an interest-free period and always pay your credit card in full by the due date

41. Never go to the automatic teller machine more than once a week, transactions cost you money

42. Avoid bank charges by having your accounts where you have your mortgage, they usually offer fee-free accounts

43. Pay your mortgage weekly or fortnightly if possible

44. Service your car regularly. You will save on repairs and create less pollution

45. If you have a mortgage have your salary paid into a mortgage offset account or redraw facility. Even if you leave it there for a week, it will help reduce your mortgage

46. Join a home exchange and swap houses with someone for holidays

47. Save by having a holiday at home, leave all those jobs that you usually do at home and do exactly what you would if you went away

48. Stop smoking or if you can't, reduce it

49. Stop gambling

50. Save the money you would normally spend on lotteries or games of chance

51. Go to the movies on discount day

52. Check the back of supermarket dockets for discounts

53. Serve smaller portions of meat and chicken and larger portions of vegetables - it may save your life

54. Take a shower. A bath uses twice as much water

55. When entertaining provide the main dish and ask your friends to bring side dishes and deserts. You do the same when you go to their house

56. Pick flowers from your garden

57. Keep bread fresher longer by putting a stick of celery in the bread box, or freeze it and take out only what you need each day

58. Prepare meals in advance and freeze them

59. Grow your own vegetables

60. Make your own entertainment by taking picnics, going for walks

The best things in life are free. We have become such a consumer-oriented society we don't seem to be aware of it any more. I know of a man who lost a lot of money. After months of unemployment he finally found work but he still had a lot of debts to repay. He constantly moaned about how he could have no social life without money but if you have friends and family, which this man had, you can make your own fun. If you have to pay to be entertained all the time you need to seriously re-evaluate your life and look at your values. Chances are, no matter how much money you have, it will never be enough.

Bread or diamonds

In simple terms the theory of bread or diamonds states that each of us has a limited income and how we choose to spend that income is up to us. We may spend our precious dollars on bread or diamonds or a combination of both. By bread I mean consumables and toys. Items such as stereos, televisions, cars and other items that depreciate and lose value over time. By diamonds I mean investments such as shares, real estate, bonds, precious gems, gold or land, all of which you hope will go up in value over time. The more

Wealth tip:
Sometimes you already have the means to achieve your goals, but because you don't expect to succeed you don't do your homework.

you spend on bread, the less there is available for diamonds. You can choose to invest in things that either go up or down in value. If you invest wisely today then your diamonds will generate enough income to buy you all the bread you will ever want tomorrow. Conversely if you spend all of your money on bread today you won't have much to show for it tomorrow.

When my children were younger they used to play with some children who lived down the street. Both the husband and wife in this family drove gold Mercedes, they wore expensive clothes and bought the best of everything. One day my children came home with gold coins that they had picked up from their friends yard. I admonished them and told them they would have to take the money back. My children replied, "Oh no it's okay, there is money lying all over the house and the back yard and they said we could keep it." A few months passed and we had this family to our place for a barbecue. They told us that they were in deep financial trouble even though their business made a lot of money. They were in trouble because they spent more than they earned. Eventually they had to sell their house and some of their prized posses-sions, simply to survive.

There will always be a reason why you can't save

Wealth tip:
Save 10 per cent of everything you earn from an early age and you will end up with a comfortable sum.

Invest 10 per cent and you could end up rich.

At each stage of life there will always be a reason why you cannot save and if you wait until the day when there is money left over it will never come. These are some of the more common reasons that people have said why they cannot save.

Teen years. When you started work you probably said, I *can't save now because I need to buy some clothes for work and to have some fun*. Then you needed CDs, a car, holidays and before you knew it you weren't able to start because you had credit card debts.

20's & 30's. In your twenties you were getting started. Maybe you had to pay for car repairs, possibly you were still paying off loans, then you had children and you had to buy furniture and baby paraphernalia.

40's & 50's. *The kids are in high school. It costs so much to live these days.* You still have the same old loans and credit card debts. The house needs repairs.

50's & 60's. *I can't save now, the kids need our help. We have to buy new appliances. The old ones are wearing out and once we are on a pension we don't know if we will ever be able to buy any large items again. Most of my superannuation will go to clearing debts. I wished I started saving when I was young.*

The most common reason that most people can't save is because they are overcommitted on credit. I have listed some smart ways to use credit but I do caution you that these will only work if you are disciplined with money and are not going to be tempted to go berserk one day on a spending spree.

Using credit wisely

The facts are, according to the July 1997 figures put out by the Reserve Bank, that Australians have $7.1 billion in credit card debt. Keep in mind that this is credit card debt only and excludes mortgages, personal loans, overdrafts and so on. It is not just the low income earners that have high levels of debt, high-income earners are notorious for spending up big on credit cards.

According to the Banking Ombudsman, who is the person to go to if you have a complaint against your bank, the main complaints about credit cards are a result of people not understanding how to read their statements and knowing the conditions of the credit card. For example any interest-free period does not apply until the outstanding balance is paid in full.

As I said before, pay all your bills, buy petrol etc. with your credit card and then make one monthly

Money brings you the ability to choose how to spend your life. I chose to stop working full time. I chose to spend more time with my family, especially with my kids.

Daniel Petrie
Chairman Kerry Packer's Internet Division

payment to your credit provider to clear the account, that way you pay no interest. Meanwhile, leave your salary in an account linked to your mortgage to reduce the interest cost on your mortgage. Many credit cards come with reward points. Use these to reward yourself for being a smart consumer.

Use your mortgage to purchase a new car. That way you get a greatly reduced interest rate and make same additional repayments off your mortgage as if you were paying a separate car loan. Better still save first.

Be wary of finance deals that appear too good to be true - they usually are. One major car company offers 100 per cent finance that has you owing just as much at the end of two years as when you purchased it. And if you have ever bought a new car, you will know just how much your car has dropped in value at the end of that time. Sure this company offers a guaranteed buy-back amount at the end of the term. All that means is that after paying for a car for three to five years you have no equity in it. Using this type of finance ensures you will be paying off a car for the rest of your life.

You will save money by buying a two year old car at auction (after shopping around and making sure you are not paying too much) and then selling it after 12 months and purchasing another car at auction. That way you will lose very little and you may even make a small profit.

If you must buy consumer items on credit pay one-third-down and the balance over 12 to 18 months, that way you minimise the interest cost.

Wealth tip:
Prosperity does not come from what you earn. It comes from what you do with what you have.

Always check, before signing, what the total cost of interest will be. Is it really worth it?

Can you pay out the loan early? Many credit providers will tell you that there is no penalty for early repayment. What they neglect to tell you is that you will still have to pay the same amount of interest whether you pay the loan out early or not.

Check if insurance is included. Many loans include insurance as well. It seems good in theory but it usually costs more than if you shopped around yourself. If you have adequate insurances then you don't really need to include extra on your loans.

Beware of rent/buy plans. They usually cost more than if you bought on a personal loan.

Leasing is no different, it is just another form of credit and usually one that is not in your favour.

Don't buy from mail order ads you see on TV unless it is something you cannot live without. Most of these items are fads, like exercise machines that you use for a few weeks and then never use again. Don't buy items on monthly payment plans that you would not pay the full amount for. Dolls are regularly advertised at $200 to $300 with the temptation of "just pay $39 a month". If you wouldn't go into a shop and pay $300 for a doll then don't be fooled by the monthly payment plan, it still costs the same.

Review your mortgage regularly as there may be better terms available. One major bank only offered a reduced rate to its existing customers if they thought they would lose them. When a customer rang for a payout figure on their loan they would offer them a better interest rate.

Be wary of interest-only loans even if using the money to buy investment property. When you depend on interest-only loans you are counting on inflation being high but what if it is not? Most people who recommend interest-only loans are people with a vested interest, like investment property salesmen who know that you can borrow more on interest-only. I like to own my properties, so I always opt for principal and interest loans.

Banks offer preferred customers lower interest rates. The better you are with your repayments and the stronger asset base you have, the better the deal you

Wealth tip:
Always look at the interest rate and total interest payable before signing.

are likely to be offered. Don't be afraid to ask.

If you overspend, use cash wherever possible and you will most likely find your spending habits will change. Most people are reluctant to part with cash but think nothing of paying with a credit card or cheque. If you tend to impulse buy, put your purchase on layby. Pay for it later with credit card so you can think about whether you really want it or not.

If it sounds too good to be true it probably is

A short while ago there were numerous advertisements for overseas credit cards. These were advertised in the major newspapers and on the Internet. One of the attractions of these cards was that they offered them to everyone. They promised no credit checks and guaranteed a card even if you had a poor credit record or were bankrupt. The credit card was only charging 4.9 per cent interest and you were guaranteed a line of credit of $4,500 immediately by paying a fee of $US100 (around $137 Australian at the time).

It all sounded too good to be true and it was. No credit cards were ever issued.

Pay out your mortgage

The greatest asset most people have is the family home. This is also where they can achieve their greatest savings, by paying off their mortgage early. For instance, if you have $5,000 sitting in a savings account paying you 3 per cent interest and you are paying 7.5 per cent on your mortgage, you are naturally going to be better off paying that money off your mortgage. If your mortgage has a redraw facility, you've got access to this money whenever you really need it.

Wealth tip:
Never go guarantor unless you are prepared to take over a loan.

Paying your mortgage weekly or fortnightly will increase the number of repayments you make each year and make a big dent in your interest cost.

Pay extra on your mortgage. Say for instance if you have a mortgage of $115,000 at 6.8 per cent over 20 years, your monthly repayments would be $877 and the total interest cost would be $95,681.

If you increased your monthly repayment by an extra $200 a month you would reduce the term of the loan from 20 years to 13.5 years and save $33,696 in interest. $200 a month could be what you normally throw away on incidentals and could be all that stands between you and financial freedom.

You can wait until your mortgage is paid off until you start working towards creating wealth but you would make more money by borrowing a small additional amount against your current property and investing in another property. That way the tenants rent would pay the mortgage off for you and there are considerable tax advantages. Obviously the sooner you start investing, the more time you have on your side to accumulate wealth. This strategy can be used time and time again to build a considerable portfolio. I have covered how to do this in more detail in chapter eleven.

The power of compound interest

Compound interest is interest on your interest. If you have $1,000 in the bank and it earns five per cent at the end of the year you will have $1,050. Next year your savings would earn interest on $1,050. How much interest you earn on your investment though can make a considerable difference to the end result.

Imagine you have $1,000 which you leave sitting in a bank account earning you 6 per cent. At the end of 30 years your $1,000 would have grown to the princely sum of $5,743. No allowance has been made for tax and you can imagine what effect inflation would have on this amount, but invest that same $1,000 in a growth type investment such as shares, and assume you averaged 15 per cent return for 30 years, your $1,000 would have grown to $66,212. This is a huge

Wealth tip:
When a bank takes care of you don't forget them. What you give out you get back.

difference just because of the interest rate. It pays to have your money working for you.

Make more money

We all want to make more money and an excellent source of income nowadays comes from network marketing. Network marketing is something that I have personally tried and can personally vouch for. I achieved company car status and a substantial income all from this source.

An added bonus to the additional income you obtain from this source are the tax write offs. If you send Christmas cards to your clients and potential clients, then the cost is tax deductible. The same applies to the use of your car, bridge tolls, postage, stationery, newspapers, street directories, and in some cases light bulbs, soap and toilet paper. If you structure your business correctly so that you have people working for you all over the country you can legitimately travel to different destinations and claim a tax deduction. It is a great way to enjoy a relaxed lifestyle that provides many tax benefits.

Consider this. How much time do you spend watching television? I can guarantee that if you stop watching television you will miss nothing of value and you will have plenty of free time to indulge in some really productive activities.

The man who does not work for the love of work but only for the money is not likely to make money nor to find much fun in life.

Charles M Schwab

Consider how you can create a second income or start a small business on the side. As the prospect of job security declines it is more important than ever to have multiple sources of income.

How many hours do you have work for $200?

The average employee works around 12 hours to make $200 and this is how much many throw away each year on their insurances. Each year I phone around and compare insurance rates because they vary all the time and each year I save $100 to $200 for my efforts. You could be throwing this much away for half an hour to an hour's work.

Most large companies have purchasing officers, and their job is to shop around to get the best prices. There is no reason that you can't do the same as some of our leading companies. Kerry Packer, Australia's richest man, only partly insures his company vehicles over a certain value. He has found it is more cost effective for his businesses to self-insure part of the cost. Every year he reviews these insurance costs in detail. Kerry Packer, despite his vast wealth, values money.

Money must circulate

It is important to understand that money is only valuable as long as it is being used. I do not recommend sticking it under a mattress. Once money has been taken out of circulation it becomes as worthless as last year's newspaper. Money that is invested in houses, shares, bonds and so on, is being used by others. Money is not meant to be taken out of circulation.

There was an old man who made his living by collecting the things that people threw out and selling them either to second-hand shops or as scrap. He lived alone and seemed to have no close relatives living near him. When he died, the authorities entered his house to take account of his possessions. Not surprisingly they found the house cluttered with old furniture and an odd assortment of collectibles from the old man's past. To their amazement however, they also found boxes packed with money. More than $200,000.

Why would some one worth over $200,000 choose to live like a pauper when he had so much at his disposal?

This man could have used his money for his own enjoyment. He could have invested it and earned a

When somebody shares, everybody wins.

Jim Rohn

return for himself or he could have helped create jobs for other people. Instead he chose to put it "in a sock under the mattress" and in doing so rendered the money absolutely useless. Money is definitely not meant to be hoarded.

Money is meant to be used, enjoyed and circulated. Remember though, keeping money in circulation does not mean squandering it.

In Summary

1. Look for ways to save money that don't affect the quality of your life.

2. Don't throw money away on things that aren't important to you.

3. Reassess your credit commitments. Is there a better way to finance them?

4. Pay off your mortgage early and start investing as soon as possible.

5. Ensure your money remains in circulation.

Chapter Six

It's time to reclaim your dream

Create a dream and give it everything you have, you could be surprised just how much you are capable of achieving. If you don't have a dream borrow one, any which way you can, you must have a dream.

Sarah Henderson

The secret to being rich and happy is to be passionate about what you do.

Thank God it's Friday! is a phrase that is muttered by people who go to work just for the money. When you work just for money the days are long, the work can be boring and most people live for the moment they can walk out that door. Not surprisingly, a recent survey confirmed that very few people want to work just for money, the main motivator for most people is enjoying what they do.

What most people do is work hard all of their life. For a lot of people this is at a job that they find mediocre, so they can retire at 60 or 65 and enjoy themselves. The problem is that when retirement comes around they usually don't have the money to do what they want. I have actually known many people who have found that they needed more money in retirement than they did when they were working. They no longer have the expenses of children and a mortgage but if they really want to live in style, travel, pursue their hobbies and lead an active social life, it costs money.

Most of us spend at least 40 hours a week at work for 48 weeks a year. Multiply that by the 40 odd years working and this adds up to 76,800 hours. Just imagine, nearly 80,000 hours of your life could be spent doing a job that you don't really enjoy.

Never work again

When you love what you do you never have to work again. Oprah Winfrey on her TV programme has often said that she loves what she does so much that she would pay to do it. When you are passionate about what you do, you ultimately reap big rewards. In Oprah's case those rewards are in excess of $40 million a year. One evening I watched an interview on TV with George Lucas. George is a director, owns a film studio and in case you didn't know, made the film Star Wars. I was fascinated to hear George say that he never sets out to make a hit movie. He makes movies because he loves doing it. He also said the same applied to his friend Stephen Spielberg, the money they make is a plus.

Now there are times in life that we have to do jobs that are not our ideal while we plan a better alternative. What most people in that position do is to focus their attention on what they don't like about their situation. And what you focus on, you get more of.

Charles Garfield tells this inspiring story in *Chicken Soup for the Soul*.[5]

Habit is either the best of servants or the worst of masters.

Nathaniel Emmons

Dr Garfield lives in America and has travelled through the 17 toll booths on the Oakland-San Francisco Bay Bridge thousands of times. Most of us know what it's like at a toll booth. We hand our toll over and hardly notice the toll collector. One day Dr Garfield was going through the toll and heard loud music. It sounded like a party or a Michael Jackson concert. The collector was dancing. Dr Garfield asked what the man was doing and the toll collector replied, "I'm having a party." As the car behind started tooting he didn't have time to ask any more questions. Months passed before Dr Garfield went through the same toll booth again and when he did, he found the toll collector still dancing. This time there was less traffic so he had time to ask more questions.

The collector described the toll booths as vertical coffins. "Each day" he said, "live people get in at 8.30 and for eight hours their brain is on hold, they are virtually dead on the job, just going through the motions". But this toll collector had attitude. He wasn't fazed by what was, because he knew where he was going. He planned to be a dancer and the way he looked at it was that his bosses were paying for him to practise on the job.

Can you imagine just how far someone with this attitude could go? This is the type of attitude that separates people who achieve their goals from those who struggle. This is a real win/win attitude that many of us would be wise to copy. Focusing on what is wrong in your job will only sap you of your energy and drive, so look for the positives. Whatever you do, do it with love.

The following list contains many of the attitudes that we experience every day. How many of them are a part of your daily life?

I don't want to get out of bed now
I don't want to start the day
I don't want to go to work
I have a short attention span
I change my mind often
I make a lot of mistakes
I'm not good at anything
I lack motivation
I have nagging doubts about my abilities
I feel bored and restless

Happy people make any work fun.

I have bad dreams and nightmares
I complain, whinge and criticise others
I often get sick, particularly during the working week
I feel tired
I worry
I am glad when Friday comes around

When you love what you do, the phone could ring at 3 a.m. and if it was someone telling you that you had just won a new contract, or got a part in a play or something really tremendous, you wouldn't care what hour of the day it was. If on the other hand you merely tolerate your work, you would feel that someone ringing you at 3 a.m. was inconsiderate and imposing on your free time.

If you have passion you can develop talent

Anne Hartley remembers wanting to write from a young age. "It wasn't a burning passion, my burning passion was to be a mother," she said, "but writing was something that I always wanted to do and always felt I was meant to do. I submitted my first short story to the Women's Weekly when I was just 10 years old. My sister and I wrote it together, not surprisingly it was rejected. At school I remember a teacher singling me out in class one day and saying, 'You think you can write don't you?' Expecting praise I nodded and she went on to say, 'Well I've got news for you - you can't'. I can remember how humiliated I felt but I also recall saying to myself, *Well I'll show you*. It was just something I always knew I would do one day. When I was in my twenties I submitted a few stories and articles to various magazines. They were all rejected. It didn't really worry me too much because I think I knew they weren't very good. At work one time I shared my dream with my boss, who was a very good writer, and he asked me to write the office manual. I was rather proud of my achievement and expected praise for my efforts. All he said was, 'Anne, forget about writing'.

Weariness usually does not come from overwork, but from lack of interest in what you are doing.

Sterling W Sill

"The truth was I was not a very good writer but for some reason I never took a writing course until much later in my career when I had already succeeded. I think I intuitively knew that too much criticism would prevent me from achieving my dream. I just knew that if this was what I was meant to do, I would find a way. Then one day when I was running a women's investment advisory business a major women's magazine asked me to write a column. I was excited as I saw this as my big opportunity. My hopes were dashed when my boss said there was no way he would allow me to write it. Instead he got our public relations consultant to write it under my name. The magazine turned the column down. I know it may seem petty but I was glad. I didn't want someone else writing under my name, this was my dream. But I also thought, *If an expert can get turned down there is hope for me yet.*

"My chance finally came one day when I was having lunch with a journalist who had at one time worked for the company I was working for. I told her how John had said there was no way I was going to write. What she said next amazed me. She said, 'Don't let that deter you. John told me I couldn't write as well and I am a journalist. Why don't you write something and I will give you an honest opinion. I can't pay you but if I like it, I'll print it in my magazine'. I wrote the article, it took me days and I had a teacher friend check it, then sent it off. My first article was published in Rydges magazine in 1984."

Since then Anne has written numerous columns for a number of major magazines, including the Women's Weekly and various newspapers. She has written three books on money, her first one reaching best-seller status within the first two months of its release. She now produces a subscriber newsletter. She combines this with her other passion of being a full-time mum.

Anne says, "Being able to share what I learn from life via my writing makes me happy. When I sit down at

Wealth tip:
If the 'why' is important enough, then no 'how' is too difficult.

my computer to write my heart sings. When I go to interview someone my heart sings. I just love it. I couldn't write at first, but I learnt by observing the alterations journalists would make to my regular columns. I knew I got those early columns because of my specialised knowledge, not my writing skills, and I wasn't too proud to learn. I worked with a wonderful team at Doubleday who published my first two books, they taught me so much. I believe wholeheartedly that if you have a strong enough desire, you can develop the talent".

Look for ways to make your job better

If you are not already in your dream job, look for ways to improve your current situation. Here are just a few suggestions that may help make your working day more enjoyable.

- Work faster and compete with yourself. See how quickly and accurately you can get through a task.

- Smile and make a point of making everyone you come in contact with a little happier.

- Aim to make each person feel special by remembering their name.

- Get up a little earlier each day and do something in your own time that will take you closer to achieving what you really want to do.

- Make a point of not repeating any gossip.

- Go out of your way to be kind to the people who really rub you up the wrong way. You will be amazed at how good you will feel when you win them over.

- Help someone else to get the job they really want.

There are no negative emotions, only negative reactions.

- Remind yourself of all that you have to be grateful for in your current situation.

When you cultivate an attitude of gratitude, even the most mundane work improves. As you change, others will take notice. Maybe an opportunity will appear in your current workplace, and if that is not what you want, it is possible that you will attract an opportunity out of the blue. Be certain of one thing, opportunities gravitate to people who are kind, co-operative and generous. There are so few that you will stand out like a beacon.

There are no coincidences

Many people give their power away to luck or coincidence. I don't believe in coincidence. We create everything with our energy.

The universe is pure energy. There is a new science called biophysics which investigates the natural energy field around the body and how it works. This is not really a new discovery, since ancient civilisations and indigenous people have always had this knowledge.

We accept such things as radios, TV, communication satellites, microwaves and computers as everyday things. They all work by transmitting energy over the airwaves, so it shouldn't be too hard to accept that our bodies transmit and receive energy in much the same way. Our bodies act as two-way radios, tuned to transmit and receive electromagnetic energy. Every part of us, every cell, every organ, every gland, every thought sends and receives at different frequencies (much like a radio station).

For instance, if fear rules your decisions, you will be tuned into that particular frequency, and you will, in turn, attract into your life others who are also fearful. We attract or repel opportunities depending on the frequency we are tuned in to; in other words when we feel optimistic we attract opportunities. When we feel fearful, we repel them.[6]

It's your choice

Unfortunately well-meaning family, teachers and counsellors often encourage young people to choose jobs that they may have an aptitude for, but are not really interested in. Many people have ended up choosing careers because of the influences of others

Whenever I set a goal I take immediate action to support it.

Anthony Robbins

or because of the money they could expect to earn. Remember, you are the one who has to go to work each day and it has to be your choice.

When I was leaving school my father wanted me to become a journalist so that I could take over his newspaper one day, but that didn't interest me. Then he wanted me to be a food technologist, saying there are always jobs in food. But I wasn't interested in that either. I was fascinated by business. I wanted to know how it worked and how to make a profit. I loved the idea of negotiating deals. My father has a gift - he had very little formal training yet he had an innate sense of business. He could work out costings on the back of an envelope and they would be remarkably accurate. I didn't inherit that gift - my approach is more traditional, although as I get older I am becoming less of an accountant and more of an entrepreneur. I told my father that I was going to study commerce and run my own business. That way I could employ people to do those other technical things for me. Because I loved what I did, I excelled at university being the only one in my class to get straight A's in every business law subject. After university I worked in a chartered accountant's office for four years to complete my final qualifications. Usually it took two years to become a senior accountant. I achieved it in one. When you love what you are doing it is easy to excel.

Nowadays my passion lies in teaching and sharing what I have learned with others. I don't work just a five day week because I love what I do. I get enormous pleasure from helping individuals turn their finances around through my education programmes and achieve real wealth and live their dreams. When you love what you are doing ultimately the money will follow.

People who feel good about themselves produce good results.

Ken Blanchard

When you don't know what you want to do

But I don't know what I want to do you may say. I've heard it many times, but I believe that intuitively we all know what we want to do. It's just that we don't always give ourselves permission to do it. Doubt stems from not believing we can have what we really want. Sometimes the dreams are so big, so far out of reach that it seems impossible to achieve. So, rather than pursuing what we think is impossible, we bury our desires deep inside, and what we really have trouble choosing is a consolation prize. Consolation prizes just don't motivate us in the same way a dream does. So we'll never have the same drive and energy to achieve it. We will never achieve all that we can by taking this path.

One way to gain clarity about your life's purpose is to look at what is important to you. These are called values and your values are a guide you can use when making decisions.

Know your values

Values are what are most important to you. They influence your decisions and they are yours to choose or to change as your life changes.

Example of values:
Freedom
Prosperity
Financial security
Social contact
Passion
Following your purpose
Marriage
Your children
Friends
Love
Fulfilment
Knowledge
Spirituality
Generosity
Creativity
Own home
Working from home

Until you start doing what you love, change your attitude so that you love whatever it is that you do.

Lisa Taylor

Knowing your values can keep you from making costly and sometimes painful mistakes. Values are another name for needs.

I said earlier that I won't do business with people whose values conflict with mine. I value integrity and ethics, so doing business with someone who does not have those values would be asking for trouble. Yet people do it every day. There is a saying, *If you lie down with dogs you get up with fleas.* You can associate, have friendships with and work with people with differing values, but if their values conflict with yours you are headed for trouble. This is particularly pertinent to the workplace. You will never find fulfilment working for someone whose values are in conflict with yours.

The same applies to relationships. Many people choose their life partner based on their personality and not their character. When the romance fades and every day conflicts arise, they discover that they have chosen to share their life with someone who has totally different values from them.

From time to time our children have asked Colette and I why we decided to get married. Our answer amazed them.

What do you value the most?

Our values influence all of our choices.

They motivate us, they determine how we are going to spend our time.

They control our decisions.

We explained that we had a mental picture of the type of person we wanted to spend the rest of our lives with. That mental image (or checklist as Colette called it) included the values, beliefs, attitudes and behaviour patterns of our perfect partner. When we found that these were compatible between us we had the basis for a good relationship. One of our values of course was love, but it wasn't the only one.

It was interesting that each of us went through this evaluation process at the time but we never really discussed it until our children first asked us about it.

Our children have commented that in their view, this was a very calculated process and that surely it's just a case of falling in love. Perhaps you might think so too.

As I said earlier, we were in love. There were other qualities however, that made this relationship special and better than previous ones we had both had. So far, we have been married almost 20 years and are still in love.

I have learnt that it is often "the little things" or incompatible values that lead to breakdowns in relationships.

Sometimes the path to personal fulfilment doesn't come clearly marked. You need to do a little searching and experimenting so that you will recognise what is important to you. Give yourself permission to have all that you can. Continue making the most of your current situation, look for opportunities and one day you will know without doubt what it is that you really want.

It's okay to change your mind

What made you happy 10, 15 years ago may not fulfil you today. As we evolve our choices change. You can change careers at any age if you believe you can.

My father loved what he did. He owned numerous businesses in publishing, distribution and the food industry. He bought a farm after suffering a heart attack but it soon became the vehicle for another business, not because he needed it, but because this was what he loved doing. His hobbies became his businesses. He was guided in all his decisions by his gut feel and he always did what he believed in.

Some people say *it's too late*, *I'm too old*, *I've missed my opportunity*. Colonel Sanders wasn't too old. If you have a burning desire, you have it for a reason.

Marianne Williamson explains this beautifully in her book A *Return to Love* [7]. She says that we often think that to follow God's will, we have to do something we

Self esteem begins to erode when your success rate drops closer to only 50 per cent.

Paul and Sarah Edwards

don't like. If you have the desire to be an actor why would God want you to be an accountant? That's not God's will. That is human conditioning.

All doubt and insecurity stems from a deep-seated belief that there is something wrong with having everything that we want. That is completely erroneous thinking. Wayne Dyer came to Australia in 1997 for the purpose of teaching that we can find happiness through having everything that we want. Unfortunately I didn't attend that seminar but those that did tell me it transformed their lives. He has certainly transformed my life through his wonderful books.

All of us have been conditioned in some way by the type of person we were expected to be and the type of life we were supposed to live. Don't underestimate the impact that many of these expectations, sometimes unspoken, have had on your choices.

Doing the impossible

Wilma Rudolph was born prematurely - the 20th of 22 children to a very poor family. When she was four, she had double pneumonia and scarlet fever that left her paralysed in her left leg. She had to wear an iron brace. The doctors told her she would never walk again, but her mother told her she could do anything she wanted.

At the age of nine, Wilma took off the leg brace and started to walk. It took her four years to develop a rhythmic stride. Then she decided she would like to be the greatest runner in the world. Can you imagine someone who couldn't even walk properly seeing themselves as being the greatest runner in the world? To most of us it would be impossible, but not to Wilma's mum.

Often in the real world, it's not the smart that get ahead but the bold.

Robert Kiyosaki

At 13 Wilma started running. She came last. She entered every race in high school and still came last. Eventually though, the day came when she won. From then on she won every race she entered. And then in the 1960 Olympic games, the impossible happened. Wilma not only won, she set a record as the first woman ever to win three gold medals.

Wilma Rudolph was not discouraged by failure or the impossible. Every time you feel discouraged by a set back or failure, remember Wilma. If you have a dream you have it for a reason. Following your dream is your purpose for living.

In Summary

1. Do what you love and you will never have to work again.

2. Develop a positive attitude to the job you have and look for ways to make it more enjoyable.

3. If you have a passion you can always develop the talent.

4. Know what you value.

5. Be grateful for all you have.

6. Follow your dream and become the best you can at it.

It's a funny thing about life;
if you refuse to accept
anything but the best,
you very often get it.

W. Somerset Maugham

Chapter Seven

Freeing the creative genius within you

Whatever you can do or dream you can, begin it.
Boldness has genius, power and magic in it, begin it now.

Goethe

Change your mindset and you can change your life.

How do you pronounce the word s-m-o-k-e?
How do you pronounce the word f-o-l-k?
What do you call the white of an egg?

Did you answer yolk? Most people do, because by using rhyming words you set up a habit pattern in the brain which assumes what the next answer will be. Actually the answer isn't yolk, the white of an egg is the albumen[8].

Even though we may think we are in charge of our lives, most of the time our actions are being ruled by patterns that we have unconsciously set up in the brain and our patterns can either support our desires or sabotage us. It doesn't mean that this pattern is right or wrong. Your automatic responses are simply the result of your life experiences.

Let me explain it this way. Most people like chocolate. When you first tasted chocolate your brain registered a pleasurable response which set off a chemical change in your body to register that feeling.

If you have only ever eaten one piece of chocolate in your life that connection would not be very strong. However, if you eat chocolate fairly regularly then your body's automatic response at the thought of eating chocolate will trigger a chemical reaction that reminds your brain that this is a pleasurable experience. The more you reinforce a behaviour or belief the stronger the pattern gets.

When you repeat a pattern, you set up a neural pathway in the brain which can start out as wispy as a single strand of a cobweb. However, after continual reinforcement it would appear more like a rope. Repetition or conditioning is what influences most of our choices and our beliefs..

Each time you let your mind dwell on something, you experience a chemical reaction in your body and that response can be pleasurable or painful.

False associations

Not all associations are correct. It's your belief in their validity that makes them true for you. For instance, if you saw your family struggle and work hard in a shop seven days a week for an ordinary income, you may have come to the conclusion that you can never make money in retail. Such a thought may send shivers down your spine. That is your reality. Someone else with different beliefs and circumstances may get a completely different response. We respond in pre-conditioned ways every day of our lives. Under extreme emotional stress we have made decisions that have set up our belief system and influenced the choices we have made. A perfect example of this is the high level of youth unemployment. Many of today's youth have made the decision that there is no point in trying to get a job because there aren't enough jobs to go around. Seeking work for some people is a painful experience. But if your conditioning had been such that you were taught that you were responsible for

Life asks of every individual a contribution and it is up to that individual to discover what it should be.

Viktor Frankl

creating your own work, rather than relying on some-one to pay you, your response would be entirely different.

The same applies to finding employment when you are over 40, 50 or any age. It is the belief in the lack of opportunities that dictates what you do and how you present yourself. Change that conditioned response. Take charge of your life and I guarantee you will find that your life will change.

I read an article in the Sydney Morning Herald[9] about people who set up their own businesses. John Furness was a paint rep and had worked for the one company for 10 years. When he was 43 years of age, John's company was taken over by a competitor and he was made redundant. John believed that there were fewer job opportunities for the over 40's and so he decided to go into business. As he had previously worked as a paint rep he decided on a paint shop.

Instead of just jumping in, John did a lot of research and learnt the basics of running a business by enrolling in the New Enterprise Incentive Scheme. This is a small business course for the unemployed, run by the Government. Three years down the track, John's small shop is turning over in excess of $200,000 a year and he is doing better than when he was an employee. John says, "They did me a favour by getting rid of me".

Your life has been shaped by the decisions you made in the past. Your future is shaped by the decisions you make today.

My father was a heavy chain smoker, I can still remember hearing his heavy coughing when I was a child. At the age of 40 my father had a heart attack and his doctor told him, "If you don't stop smoking imme-diately, I'll see you in Rookwood" (a large cemetery in Sydney). My father came home, gathered up all his cigarettes and threw them in the bin. He is now 77 and has not smoked a cigarette since that day.

The belief comes first - success follows.

It took enormous will power and was not easy. Because smoking is addictive, he suffered withdrawal symptoms for quite some time. But he had made his decision to stop and that was that. Thoughts are creative. He created a smoke-free life from that day on.

When a neural pathway is no longer used, it withers and eventually dies. If you were a chocaholic and you stopped eating chocolate, after a while you would stop craving it. The same applies to any habit we want to change such as smoking, eating, drinking, gambling and spending. If you want to eliminate anything from your life you just stop doing it, it is as simple as that.

Well, it sounds simple, but if you have ever tried to diet and failed or given up smoking only to take it up again, you know that a strong connection is hard to break if you don't have the motivation. Motivation is vitally important because it is what makes change easy. For my father, the consequences of continuing to smoke were so dire that his motivation to give it up was stronger than his old pattern.

Genius is nothing but a great capacity for patience.

Georges-Louis Buffon

Find a dream that you really, really want. Do whatever you need to do to motivate yourself sufficiently to make permanent changes to your attitude and habits and you will find the change effortless. That is why we set goals.

Viktor Frankl, in his classic book *Man's Search for Meaning* , wrote of life in a concentration camp during World War II. He calculated that only one person in 28 survived the horror of the camps and he made a personal study as to why one man would survive while many others perished.

He observed that the person who survived was not necessarily the fittest, healthiest, the best-fed or the most intelligent. What he found was that those who made it through had a reason to keep going. They had a GOAL. In Frankl's case, his burning desire was to see his wife's face again. Other survivors had different goals, but all had major goals nevertheless.

Goals are what keep us going. I've often heard of people dying within a year after retirement. Once we lose our momentum, once we lose our direction, we are in trouble!

Wishy washy goals are not going to motivate you. I have heard people say, *Well, I'd like to save* $10,000. Well, saving $10,000 may motivate you but I doubt it has enough pulling power to make a strong connection. Make your goal more powerful. What will financial freedom give you? Do you want to travel? Do you want your children to have a private school education? Do you want to live in the house of your dreams? Do you want to work at your dream job? Do you want to never worry about money again? These are all powerful goals but whatever you choose, make sure that what you choose excites you enough to put in the effort to achieve it or you won't make it. You need to see it clearly, feel it, smell it, taste it, hear it. Have a strong image of your goal in your mind and recall it often.

Wealth tip:
Act as if it is impossible to fail.

Sue and Peter whose story I told in chapter three, both knew that they had to change or their marriage was in danger. That was enough to motivate them into making choices that would turn their lives around. Some people have to hit bottom before they have sufficient motivation to make a change. Hitting rock bottom is not the worst thing that can happen to you. Giving up is the worst.

I am saying to you that it is never too late. You are in the right place at the right time and your best opportunities are before you right now. Of course, there will always be people who tell you that you've missed the boat, it's too late, all the opportunities are gone. Absolute rubbish! You can turn any situation around when you make the decision to do so. The choice is yours. You can do it easily if you are motivated enough. If not, you may need to use some discipline and will power.

To overcome the fear of failure, you need a goal that is worth failing for. Your goals have to make you burn with desire. Your goals must be emotional.

The reality is though, that very few people set financial goals beyond a house and car. Once you achieve a goal, set another, and use the enormous power of your mind to support you in designing a life.

You can do this by using specific techniques that will reinforce the belief that you can have what you want. Elite athletes use such methods constantly to help them set new records. You are a financial athlete in training and you need to support your goals with positive self talk.

Reprogramming the subconscious mind

Your subconscious mind is much like a computer. A computer cannot think, feel, or create. It presents back to you what has been programmed into it. The difference is that a computer can access resources in seconds that would take you days, weeks and even months of research to find. Your subconscious is just like the computer. Give it an order and it will go and

Dreams are what lead us to our destiny.

Anne Hartley

find it for you.

You have been conditioned all of your life by other people. First it was your parents, then teachers, your peers and finally the media. Often many of the beliefs that you hold in your subconscious are not what you would choose for your life today, but the fact is that these beliefs are what is running your life.

In order to create what you want, you need to reprogram your computer and you do this through the conscious mind. The conscious mind has two distinct control centres. The left side of the brain controls memory, speech, logic and rational thinking. The left side of the brain thinks in words so you reprogram it with your words. These are called affirmations.

Affirmations

An affirmation is a positive statement of fact not hope. If you want to be financially independent you would not say, *One day I will be financially independent*, or, *in the year* 2000 *I will be financially independent*. What does financially independent mean to you? Does it mean that you own your own home, that you own an investment portfolio, that you pay your bills easily and effortlessly? Be specific and state your affirmation as if it were already fact. You could say, I *am a home owner*, or I *have a million dollar investment portfolio*. Remember that your mind is a computer, it doesn't decide if you are right or not. It believes anything you tell it, so tell it what you want, not what you don't want.

In the beginning of this book I mentioned how people constantly say what they don't want such as, I *can't afford it*. These statements work the same as affirmations and what you constantly say becomes your reality. It does take effort at first to establish a new habit, but that is all it is. By taking the time to establish a positive habit where all of your statements are in effect positive affirmations, you will transform your life and your circumstances.

Wealth tip:
If you want to rise above being average you need to reassess the way you think about and handle money. Do your habits support your dreams?

I preface my affirmations with, I *am so happy that* I *am/have…* For me this reinforces the pleasure that I will enjoy when I achieve the goal and also makes me grateful for the wonderful things I have in my life.

I have heard people say, *Well I am very positive but my husband (or wife) is constantly complaining (or holding me back or whatever)*. Sorry, that is your excuse for not changing. You are responsible for the thoughts that circulate in your mind. You are responsible for the words that come out of your mouth, no-one else is. Your partner has the right to choose to stay exactly where they are. If you want to change then you need to work on yourself. It is harder, I agree, but it is essential that you take responsibility for your situation personally in order to change it.

For some people responsibility has negative connotations. I see responsibility as the key to freedom. If you accept responsibility for where you are now, you also have the power to make new decisions which will change where you will be in the future.

An affirmation repeated over and over will set up a neural pathway in your brain. However, an affirmation said with emotion will work much faster for you. Think about a time in your life when you felt particularly emotional about something. There may be a particular song that triggers a happy memory or a sad feeling when you hear it. Doesn't that feeling come back to you? This is what you are doing when you say your affirmations. Feel them, sing them, associate good feelings with them. Get excited about the changes that are coming your way. Imagine what it will be like when you have all that you want. Got the picture? Remember your subconscious is an order taker. It does not know the difference between fact and fiction. If you tell it you already have what you want, it believes you and goes seeking ways to bring all that you desire into your life.

Responsibility leads to freedom

Visualise your life the way you want it to be

Just as the left side of the brain thinks in words, the right side of the brain sees images. The right side is the creative centre that controls rhythm and movement and our artistic ability. Most people are left brain dominant but we develop the right side of the brain by using visualisation techniques. You may think why bother, because for some people seeing pictures in their mind is a difficult process, but you need to develop this centre as it is the source of your creativity. Think of it as a muscle that has not been used for a long time. At first you have to work at getting it into condition but it will develop, it just takes practise. And as I keep asking my children, how do you get good at something? Practise! Practise! Practise!

The aim is to see the object that you desire in your mind as if you already have it. For instance, if you want to have a better home or your first home, then imagine it. Walk through the rooms. What colour are the walls? How big is the garden? Put in all those little things that are important to you. Maybe you like lots of light and storage, maybe you want a pool and privacy from your neighbours. Do not imagine what you can afford which may be a run down shack. That may be what you are planning to buy but see it the way that you want it to look. Athletes don't imagine themselves falling down and failing. They see themselves crossing over the finishing line, being first, winning a gold medal, being the best.

You can bring your other senses into play as well. For example, smell the roses in your garden, hear your friends congratulating you, taste those fresh home-grown vegetables. Use as many of your senses as you can to enable your mind to accept that your goals are already reality.

Take a quiet time each day, it doesn't have to be long, possibly 10 minutes or so to just sit quietly and imagine your life the way you want it to be. Imagine what you will do each day. You may be working in your own business or decorating your new home. Maybe you are somewhere overseas shopping in Italy, skiing in Switzerland or having fun with your family at Disneyland. Make the picture as vivid as you can, bring in colours, emotions, smell the smells, hear the crowds around you.

Visualisation can bring about physical change. Muscle activity measured during a session of visualising intense physical exercise showed that the muscles actually respond to what the mind conceived.

A lot of people know of these techniques. They are not new, but how many people practise them on a daily basis? It never ceases to amaze me that the very people who are happy to spend hours moaning about the way things are will not take 10 minutes a day to control their destiny. That is why so few people are living their dream.

Isn't your dream worth just 10 minutes a day?

In life lots of people **know** what to do, but few people actually do what they know. Knowing is not enough. You must take action. Before you dismiss this information by saying you have heard it all before, let me caution you that the reading and understanding of this information on an intellectual level is not going to change your life. Neither will memorising it give you the success you desire. You don't know something until you actually do it for yourself. You do not understand something until you can explain it to someone else so that they can understand it. Please think about this deeply.

Even if you have heard it all before, unless you are actually applying it in your life right now, take time out to practise them. Consistently apply these methods for at least 30 days and your life will never be the same again!

In Summary

1. What you believe may not be true for everyone.

2. Use your words to create new beliefs.

3. Visualise your life the way you want it to be.

4. You can create your own reality.

*The only way to discover the limits of
the possible is to go beyond them,
to the impossible.*

Arthur C. Clarke

Chapter Eight

The games people play

Those who know the truth learn to love it.
Those who love the truth learn to live it.

Bob Proctor

You can never get enough of what you don't really want

I know a man who lost all his money when his business failed. He was aged 45 at the time. It's not pleasant and in fact I imagine it could be downright demoralising. If he had been prepared to start again he could have saved and bought another home again and built on that, but he considered that beneath him. Instead he paid a high rent to live in the same area where he had previously lived because he refused to lower his standards. He worked two jobs just to keep up an image, drove a car that was more than he could afford and sent his children to private schools. He was always waiting for his ship to come in. He just knew one day he would make it big.

At one time I suggested to this man that he rent in a cheaper area not far from his home so that he could save a deposit to buy a low-cost investment property and build on that. The area I suggested he move to is not far from where he lives and is certainly very pleasant, but he replied, "I would not lower myself. I would rather die first."

By retirement age this man's net worth was zero and he had to continue working at a job that he disliked. All because he thought he had to live up to an image. Eventually there will come a day when this man won't be able to work any more and then the prospects for him and his family look grim. This is false pride and no-one can help him until he is prepared to help himself.

A rage against the ordinary

There are many people like this man who would fit into the category that Barbara Sher, author of *I could do Anything If I Only Knew What It Was* [10], describes as having a rage against the ordinary.

Barbara asks these questions:

Do you live beyond your means, financially, emotionally, or some other way?

Do you have a big dream or two that never quite comes through?

Do you make promises you can't keep?

Are a lot of people mad at you?

Are they tired of helping you?

Do you feel furious and misunderstood?

Unlike those who don't know what they want from life, a rager knows exactly what he wants. He dreams big dreams and is often angry, even though he may bury it deep inside when thing don't go the way he wants. Ragers are often very talented. They certainly are not lazy and often have very charismatic personalities. To quote Barbara who explains this so well:

'Just a minute,' you might be saying. 'What about Michaelangelo and Muhammad Ali and everyone else who ever accomplished extraordinary things? Did they settle for drab,

As incomes increase, it takes more and more money to 'buy' the degree of expressed happiness experienced before the increase.

Robert Lane

workaday lives? Big winners need to take big risks, don't they?' Am I suggesting we waddle passively, like lemmings, into an abyss of mediocrity?

Of course not.

But ragers have made a serious miscalculation. They've missed the difference between raging against the ordinary and being extraordinary. An extraordinary life, a life filled with great accomplishments, is also filled with a myriad of very mundane details, hard work, and patience. Famous scientists have to pay their electric bills and walk their dogs. Successful actors have to stand in line at the supermarket. Everybody's day-to-day life is ordinary.

Extraordinary people don't waste any energy raging against the ordinary - they don't even care about what's ordinary and what's not. They're too busy taking one small step after another. You may be a prodigy, born with a whole range of talents, but the more gifted you are, the harder and longer you must work to create something that matches your vision. Talent plus patience will allow you to master your craft - and mastery is what gets you your dream.

Why do you want it?

Knowing why you want your desires can save you from wasting a lot of time and frustration. Stephen Covey says that sometimes we are so focused on climbing the ladder of success, only to find out that once we reach the top, the ladder is actually leaning against the wrong wall.

Helen was very successful in business. She set goals religiously and achieved most of them. She was well respected in her industry. Then one day she walked away from it all. Helen said, "What I really wanted from my work was recognition and I achieved everything that I set out to achieve, but the public recognition did not fulfil me and the work I was doing was not what I really wanted to do. What I was searching for in those days was not recognition but to be valued".

Those who bring sunshine to the lives of others cannot keep it from themselves.

J.M. Barrie

119

Helen left her job and all the trappings that went with it and settled for less financially in order to be able to do work that she really loved. "I know some people may think I'm crazy," she said, "but I realised that no-one else could fill my emotional needs. If I want others to value me then I have to do it for myself, and for me that means being true to myself by doing what I really want, even if that means making less money in the short term. My life has changed quite dramatically. A lot of people have gone from my life, I think some of them look on me as a has been, but many wonderful new friends have entered. I really respect myself and I like who I am. Most importantly, I am happy."

Logan Pearsall Smith said that, "There are two things to aim at in life: first, to get what you want; and, after that, to enjoy it."

This book is not just about achieving riches because many do that and are miserable. You can never get enough of what you don't really want.

When ego runs our lives, then we always have to have something or be something in order to be fulfilled. Ego is another name for fear, because the ego does not feel safe unless it is in control. Ego is very reactive and its prime concern is what other people will think. Wayne Dyer explains this in his book, *Your Sacred Self*[11]:

> When you spend time and energy concerned about how others are viewing you, you are in the clutches of your ego. Fear will be your constant companion. A focus on fear is the vehicle that you use for the expression of your humanity. The vehicle is the career you have chosen, the clothes you wear, the possessions you have accumulated, the money you have and all the ways you are expressing yourself.

> These vehicles can become the real focus of your life. They are attempts to let the world and yourself know how important you are and to satisfy your ego's insistence on recognition.

Wealth tip:
Make sure your work improves the world in some way.

A focus on love does not concern itself with needing to impress or with the external status symbols of your life. Love is expressed in the service of God and in the service of others.

Focusing on love and being of service does not mean giving up your dreams, far from it. There is nothing wrong with wanting the good things in life. If up until now your goals have been set for the approval from others, then all you need to do is to change your motivation from one of getting to one of giving.

This means a shift in your focus from, *What's in it for me*, to *How can I serve*? Rather than saying, *How can I get more customers*, you ask, *How can I provide a better service in my business*? Instead of, *How can I get more out of my staff* turn it into, *How can I make my employees or co-workers feel good about themselves and what they do*?

We can do more for others when we have more

You can do more to change the world by having money than by being one of the crowd. When you accumulate wealth you can buy property. This way you are able to provide homes for people who need them. If there weren't any landlords there would not be enough homes for people who rent. When you invest in shares you are providing funds for companies to grow, create jobs and provide services and goods to us all.

No man is an island and what we do affects everyone else as a whole. The process of writing a book involves a whole range of people from editors, graphic designers, typesetters, printers, delivery people to the people who work in the bookshops. This list could go on and on. All work, even the most menial work can be of service to others.

You will feel far more fulfilled by the achievement of your dreams when you give to others. Not only that you will go further and make more money. It does not

Thou shalt decree a thing and it shall be established unto thee.

Job 22:28

121

matter if you are an employee or own your own business, anyone stands out from the crowd when they develop an attitude of service. Service is what is lacking in this country. Service is what can make you mega rich.

Our work and the goals that we pursue are a part of our purpose, our reason for being. Make your life one of service to others and you cannot help but prosper.

John Wooden said, "You can't live a perfect day without doing something for someone who will never be able to repay you."

In Summary

1. All men are equal.

2. Know why you want your goals. You don't need to change your goals but you may want to change your motivation if they are ego driven.

3. You can do more when you have more.

4. Your work is a part of your purpose.

Chapter Nine

Money and spirituality

Ask, and you will receive;
seek, and you will find;
knock, and the door will be opened to you.

Matthew 7:7

Money is power. Use it to help all mankind.

Money and spirituality go hand in hand,. They are not in conflict with each other. Since the beginning of time many well-meaning people have let opportunities slip through their fingers because they believed that having a lot of money is wrong. Money of itself is nothing - what we do with money is what makes it a positive tool or a negative tool.

I believe strongly that each one of us is responsible for creating what we want and God gives us the tools to do this. The last thing that God wants is for people to end up in their old age looking to someone else to support them.

Take the parable of the three servants (Matthew 25:14). A man called together his servants before embarking on a long journey. To one he gave $10,000, another $4,000 and the other $2,000. He then left them to take care of his property. The servant who received $10,000 went and invested it and doubled his master's money. The servant who received $4,000 did the same. But the servant who received $2,000 dug a hole in the ground and buried it.

When the master returned he called his servants to him and asked them to settle their accounts. The first two servants gave their master back $20,000 and $8,000 respectively and their master said, "Well done, good and faithful servants, you have been faithful in managing small amounts, so I will put you in charge of large amounts. Come on in and share my happiness!" The third servant explained to his master that he was afraid and buried the money in the ground, to which the master responded, "Now take the money away from him and give it to the one who has $20,000, and he will have more than enough; but the one who has nothing, even the little he has will be taken away from him."

If you don't look after what you have then you will lose it. Money brings with it the responsibility to use it for the good of all and it can be a valuable tool. Why then do so many with high moral values allow power to be taken from them by not pursuing what they want? Why too do people complain about the lack of ethics in big business, but do nothing about changing the situation?

I read an article recently which said that Bill Gates, the world's richest man, intends accumulating his money for the next 10 years, then he plans to give it all away. I don't know if this is true or not, or whether it will happen. Imagine though what an impact Bill Gates, the philanthropist, could make on the world. Would you not prefer the power for change to be in the hands of those who would do the greatest good?

Experience is a hard teacher because she gives the test first, the lesson afterwards.

Vernon Law

Money is a source of power. There is no doubt about that and by utilising this power you too can have a tremendous impact on mankind. If more well-meaning people would reclaim their power by using money for the greater good of all, they would achieve more than by walking away and declaring money to be the source of all evil, and criticising and envying those with money.

God doesn't want us to be poor. Some people use God as an excuse for not taking responsibility for their financial affairs. They say, *God will look after us*. Or, *I'm waiting for a sign from God*. Ask for a sign by all means but don't wait too long because God helps those who help themselves.

The best thing you can do for the poor is not to be one of them. You can't give away what you haven't got.

What is your purpose in life?

This is a question that only you can answer.

We find true happiness when we follow our purpose. You cannot live your purpose without healthy self esteem. Self esteem is just another way of saying that you value yourself.

I was driving home last night and as I travelled down a well known main road I passed a group of very young, very pretty girls working as prostitutes. It started me thinking that lack of self esteem is at the core of all society's problems. If everyone valued themselves highly enough and knew they could have what they wanted they would not have to sell their bodies or resort to gambling, drugs or crime.

Poverty is a mental disease that stems from low self esteem. Like many diseases, it is curable for those who believe it can be. As with any illness, it takes effort, initiative and courage to beat it - and if you give up, you're in trouble!

The good news is that nearly all happy and prosperous people have conquered this debilitating mental disease at some time in their lives.

The higher your self esteem, the more you can allow into your life.

I constantly ask the question, "How can I add value to people's lives?" Through this thought process, I became a leader.

Anthony Robbins

A new book on the market, *Conversations with God*[12], by Neale Donald Walsch explains the paradigm that many have about taking money for work that is their higher calling. The following excerpt is a portion of the answer that Neale received when he asked God why he always struggled with money:

Most people do what they hate for a living, so they don't mind taking money for it. "Bad" for the "bad" so to speak. But you love what you do with the days and times of your life. You adore the activities with which you cram them.

For you, therefore, to receive large amounts of money for what you do would be, in your thought system, taking "bad" for the "good" and that is unacceptable to you. You'd rather starve than take "filthy lucre" for pure service...as if somehow the service loses its purity if you take money for it.

So your life with regard to money is going to go in fits and starts, because you keep going in fits and starts.

The only way to change such a situation is to change how you think about it. Give yourself permission to follow your highest calling and be paid abundantly for it.

What motivates you?

In our efforts to be all that we can be, there are two types of motivation. One is the deficiency motivation. You can look at yourself and the world at large and decide what is wrong with it. Your desire to change is a need to fix things so that they match your mental image of what they should be. Or, you can be motivated to change because you want to expand and grow and be all that you can be. Both will work, but my experience has been that you will be happier and more fulfilled by focusing on being all that you can be, rather than trying to fix what is wrong.

We must learn to help those who deserve it, not just those who need it. Life responds to deserve, not need.

Jim Rohn

Self esteem goes beyond feeling good about yourself. It is about believing in yourself and your ability to give and receive, in other words make a valuable contribution. If you get into the habit of asking yourself at the end of each day, D*id I make a contribution today?* You will soon become aware of what your specific purpose is.

In making a contribution to the world you will discover your spiritual connection. I found that once I discovered my purpose, I felt incredibly powerful and that everything just fell into place. I take this as confirmation that I am doing, what I am meant to be doing. Information, guidance and help is always available to us but it depends on how receptive we are to receiving it.

Robert Allen says, "Purpose is knowing what you want and doing it because it expresses who you really are".[19]

When you think about people who are masters of anything you will usually find they are passionate about it. Imagine Greg Norman not playing golf, Elton John not singing or writing music, or Mother Theresa not helping the poor. Mother Theresa particularly was a shining example. She did not have to serve the poor. She came from a wealthy family, she chose that life because she was passionate about ending the suffering of others. Passion is the fuel which keeps you going even when the going gets tough. Having a higher purpose, a reason beyond just acquiring is what makes pursuing goals such fun.

Ask and you shall receive

Ask yourself these questions:

What do I love to do?

What do I feel passionate about?

What would I do if money were no object?

How would I live my life if I only had six months to live?

What motivated me to make sacrifices in the past?

If you want what you're asking me for with all your heart, then there's nothing I can do to stop you from getting it.

Andrew Carnegie

127

How can I contribute?

What always seems to work out for me?

The purpose of these questions is to assist you in finding what makes you come alive. What makes your heart sing at this time in your life? The Bible does not say, ask and maybe you will receive. The message is very clear, **ask and you will receive.** Have you ever thought that you may have your desires for a valid reason?

The late Dr Spock, well-known author on many books about how to raise children said that he became a paediatrician because he loved children. He became an author because he wanted to teach parents how to raise healthier children. He fought against nuclear weapons because he hated the thought of what war does to children. As you evolve so too will your purpose.

From purpose to intention

It's tempting to say, Well, *if God wants me to do this he will find a way.* Sorry, that doesn't work. Unless you take responsibility for creating what you want God won't do it for you. You can say you are 'gunadoo' this and 'gunadoo' that but you will never get around to it until you take action.

Let's say your purpose is to help others. It's a nice purpose but it lacks power. How are you going to do it? You could expand your purpose and make it a goal that could be, I *will own my own business that will provide employment for youth and I will give away 10 per cent of all my profits.* Better, but still not powerful enough.

Be specific. What type of business do you want? Who will you give your money to? How will you assist youth? What type of training programmes will you provide? When will you start?

A man with heart is someone who remains faithful until there is no more hope. Desperation is cowardice.

Euripides

128

The less you need, the more you can have

Life is a paradox because the less you need anything, be it money, success, love or the achievement of your goals, the more likely you are to achieve them. Remember money is merely a tool and the only power it has is what you bestow upon it.

When you hold on to what you want too tightly, you can become fearful and fear prevents us from making wise decisions. When you can hold what you want in an open hand knowing that abundance is your right, then you will ultimately take action that will bring more of what you want into your life. Fear repels money and opportunity - trust attracts it.

In Summary

1. Know why you want your goals.

2. Have a purpose for living that is a powerful motivating force.

3. Focus on giving rather than receiving.

4. Accept that you can be spiritual and wealthy. It is okay to be paid abundantly for doing God's work.

I never threw money around. I learned from my father that every penny counts, because before too long your pennies turn into dollars. To this day, if I feel a contractor is overcharging me, I'll pick up the phone, even if it's only for $5,000 or $10,000, and I'll complain. People say to me, 'What are you bothering for, over a few bucks?' My answer is that the day I can't pick up the telephone and make a twenty-five cent call to save $10,000 is the day I'm going to close up shop.

Donald Trump

Chapter Ten

Never fight about money again

*Doing the same things over and over again
and expecting a different result is insane.*

Anthony Robbins

**When you look for a solution rather than focus on
the problem you will find a way.**

Fights over money are one of the major causes of
marital problems. However, this issue is not just exclu-
sive to husband and wife. It can cause conflict in the
workplace and in some instances between parents and
children.

There can be many reasons for these problems.
They could be because of differing values, power struggles or the result of differing belief systems. Whatever
the source of conflict is, you would do well to eliminate it from your life, but walking away from a
situation does not necessarily end the problem. There
are many divorced people who still fight over money.
The Family Law Court is filled to overflowing with
disputes on property settlements. There are also many
divorced women who still give their power away to
their ex-husbands by allowing them to control their
finances.

You end conflict by taking responsibility for yourself. The common belief is that it is harder to achieve financial goals if one party sabotages your plans. It is also a widely held belief that it is difficult to achieve financial goals as a single person, such as a house, particularly if you have children. It can be harder and many struggle with this issue but it doesn't have to be when you learn to develop your creativity. Let me say here that very few people are born naturally talented, most of us develop our talents because of necessity.

When you look for a solution rather than focusing on the problem you will find a way.

Divorce your finances

How can I become wealthy when my husband constantly spends?" said Jenny. "I only work part-time because I want to spend time with my children. I just can't see how it is possible".

When you believe in lack and limitation, it is easy to look at your circumstances and if you cannot find an obvious answer, decide there is no way out. I don't believe that. In this instance, Jenny and her husband had to sell their home. They were overcommitted with debts because her husband is a compulsive spender. Jenny scrimps and saves and manages to save a little from the household budget but it will be a long time before Jenny will have a decent sum to invest and multiply.

Jenny and Paul's differing values are a constant source of conflict for them and left unresolved could ultimately destroy their relationship. It is hard to be in a loving relationship with someone who is constantly undermining you. In Jenny and Paul's case I suggested that they end this dichotomy by divorcing their finances.

Wealth tip:
The most important way to ensure success in any relationship is to communicate clearly up front.

"Well, that's great in theory," Jenny responded to my suggestion angrily, "But just how am I supposed to manage when Paul is the major income provider?"

If Jenny and Paul were to divorce in the practical sense they would divide up their assets and Paul would be required to pay child support to Jenny for the upkeep and welfare of their children. I suggested they do the same thing by dividing up Paul's income and each person being responsible for their own commitments.

Paul and Jenny amicably worked out their main areas of concern with money and looked for possible solutions. They decided to transfer the car into Jenny's name. She was constantly worried about the threat of repossession as Paul sometimes skipped payments. This cost a small amount in stamp duty but to Jenny it was worth the peace of mind. Paul became responsible for their credit card debts. Although Jenny received an amount each week for housekeeping, Paul decided to increase this as she took over the car payments, rent and major expenses such as electricity and telephone. Paul was responsible for all repair work, medical, dental, presents and clothes. These were the areas in which Paul was happy to spend.

We all seek a solution that will end all of our problems forever. Sometimes it takes time and experimentation to find a way that suits both of you. Paul continued to overspend and Jenny had to learn to let go of her expectations of Paul and accept him as he is. We can hope another will change but we can't expect it, not if you want harmonious relationships. For the day-to-day management of their affairs this system worked quite well for them with some minor adjustments. But there was still not enough money left over with which to buy a house or accumulate wealth.

It took a while for Jenny to accept that she was responsible for setting her own goals and achieving them. Paul simply didn't care whether they owned a home or not. Jenny did. So Jenny set about creating work that would provide her with a good income and still allow her to be at home with her children.

Wealth tip:
People with high self esteem make their own choices, they are in control.

When we are clear about what we want, opportunities gravitate to us. A lot of success in life just happens when you are in the right frame of mind. I'd like to share with you a story that I told Jenny about Susie O'Neil. Susie dreamed of a safer world for kids and she dared to dream the impossible.

Creating opportunities

At 34, Susie, a former pre-school teacher and mother of four ventured into a new business called Kids Construction Inc[13]. She financed the business from the sale of her car and still runs the business from their property in Ballarat.

Realising that most of the material on safety for children was outdated, Susie sat down and created eight animated cartoon characters such as Pippa the painter (sun safety), Bobby the brickie (sports safety) and Peter the plumber (water safety). Coming up with a unique idea such as Susie's is wonderful, but sadly there are many talented people who die poor. Susie was able to turn her dream into reality by asking for help. She did this by sending out 100 letters outlining her idea to marketing managers of very large companies. Out of 100 letters she got six appointments. She persisted until she found someone who would listen to her ideas. One of the companies that listened was Mitre 10 who developed the concept with Susie.

Susie now licenses her cartoon characters to Tontine, SPC, Mitre 10, Target, Decor, Bostick and Nestle to name a few. She also produces a magazine called Kelly Street, which is distributed free in Victoria to school children. It's central theme is safety, and there are numerous other projects underway.

Wealth tip:
Never let anyone tell you it can't be done when you know in your heart it can.

Susie's business is conducted in a separate building on their property but Susie is still available for her children. Susie says, "Once I get an idea I remain focused and follow through."

Inspired by Susie's success Jenny reassessed her

strengths and skills. Her main skills were in the secretarial area and Jenny wondered if she could possibly start by doing typing at home. The problem was, she didn't know how to get clients. Even though they had a computer Jenny didn't have any money to buy a business or to spend on advertising. There were times when Jenny would lament, "I'm not an entrepreneur, I just want to be a mum." Jenny was also aware that she had to make choices. If she chose to just stay at home, then it was highly unlikely that she would have her own home and they would never have any of the things that really mattered to her. She also worried about the example they were setting for their children.

Reclaiming your power

Jenny's opportunity came one day quite by chance, as most opportunities do, when she took one of her children to see an eye specialist. During a long wait to see the doctor she overheard the receptionist say a number of times how much work she had and how behind she was with the typing.

The next day Jenny rang a number of doctors' offices in a specialist centre located near her home. She explained that she was just researching at this time and asked them if they would use an outside typing service for their overload work. Many of them said they would. A major drawback was that Jenny did not know medical terminology. After more research she discovered that she could buy software for her computer and a hard cover medical dictionary for $80. This was within her means.

Taking courage in her hands she rang the eye specialist's office and spoke to the practice manager. She told them that she wanted to learn medical terminology and offered to work in their office as a typist during school hours on a voluntary basis for two weeks if they would help her with the terminology. They jumped at the opportunity.

Wealth tip:
Value your stay-at-home spouse by paying them a wage.

135

Jenny said, "It was like learning a foreign language at first but as I am a good speller I was able to pick it up fairly easily. The practice manager at the eye specialist's office was so impressed with my approach that she contracted all their typing to me on a regular basis, which was about 10 hours work a week. I found out that the going rate for medical typing was $25 an hour, far more than I could make working part-time. I made up my own flyer on the computer and dropped it into other offices in the building. With the recommendation that I received from my first client, I soon had more work than I could handle".

After two years Jenny sold off part of her business and with these proceeds she had a deposit for a home. Jenny said, "Divorcing our finances was the best thing that we ever did. We no longer fight about money and I realise that there is always a way for Paul and I to have what we both want. I bought our home, which is in my name. It's not that I don't want to share it with Paul, it really belongs to both of us but with Paul's spending habits I would always worry that we would lose it again. He agreed with this. Although Paul still gives me the same amount that we previously paid in rent, I now combine that with the same amount from my typing business. That way we should be able to pay the house off in 10 years and then I am going to invest.

"For me the single most important lesson that I learned, is that I am responsible for me. Paul and I accept each other more and our children don't have to listen to us fighting about money any more. In fact, next year Paul is taking us all to Disneyland. He loves these extravagant gestures and I love him for it. Now I know we can afford it. In fact, for the first time in my life I know that I can have everything that I want. What a turnaround in just two years!"

Wealth tip:
Listen to what people complain about and you will always find an opportunity for making money.

If you depend on another person to provide you with everything you want you give your power away.

There is always a way to have what you want in a way that you want it.

A friend of mine, Lance Spicer, teaches businesses how to save tax by setting up overseas corporations. He is often in demand as a public speaker. Lance does not enjoy speaking in public especially in front of large groups. To take advantage of this opportunity Lance asked his clients if they would be happy to show a video of him explaining these structures rather than him appearing personally and they agreed. He had a video made where he talked in the comfort and familiarity of his own living room. Whenever he is asked to speak, he gives his clients the video instead and is paid handsomely for this service. There is always a way when you give yourself permission to have what you want.

In Summary

1. You are responsible for achieving your own goals.

2. If money is a source of conflict in your relationship, divorce your finances.

3. Reclaim your power by acting on opportunities when they present themselves.

4. Remember, where there is a will, there is always a way.

A creditor is worse than a slave-owner; for the master owns only your person, but a creditor owns your dignity, and can command it.

Victor Hugo

Chapter Eleven

Understanding Money

When you have a wealth plan, you'll be so motivated that you'll have a hard time going to bed at night.

Jim Rohn

Your assets will feed you, while your liabilities will eat you.

Financial literacy is the one subject that separates the poor and middle class from the rich, but understanding the money game does not have to be hard. Before you begin to learn the basics of making money let me explain the difference between the rich and the poor.

Habits of the rich and poor

The poor go to work to earn money, pay taxes and spend the rest. It is not that they necessarily earn low incomes, but all of their money goes towards the latest consumer toys. When they are not buying toys, they are usually eating, drinking, smoking or gambling their money away. They live from week to week.

The middle class go to work, pay taxes and they spend. They buy a home, add a pool, move up to a bigger house, buy new furniture, put a little into super-annuation or a savings plan. Their budgeting habits may ease financial pressure but they do not make them rich.

The rich go to work, spend their money to build an asset base and then pay taxes on the rest. The rich often pay less tax than the poor because they know how to play the money game.

The poor and middle class go to work to make money and if they lose their job, their financial security usually goes out the door as well. If they are unemployed for any length of time their whole asset base is threatened. When you go to work just for money, you are working for the Taxation Department. If you have a mortgage and consumer debt you are also working for the bank and credit providers.

The rich don't work for money. They may go to work for fun, they may even have a job, but their main source of income is their asset base. If their income goes up, their taxes don't necessarily follow because of strategies they have already put in place. In other words their assets are working for them. The rich may or may not budget, but many of them use the 80/20 plan.

The 80/20 plan

The 80/20 plan means that the first 10 per cent of all you earn you give away. Some people like to give it back to God, others like to give it to charity, while others just like to give it to wherever they feel led to give. Imagine a world where everyone gave 10 per cent back to helping and supporting each other. We could totally eliminate poverty in one generation.

I make sensible business decisions. I am very conservative in business. People don't think that because of my public persona.

Rene Rivkin

The next 10 per cent you give to yourself by allocating this money to building an asset base that will one day support you. You may put these savings in a bank account until you accumulate around $5,000 and then invest in income and growth investments.

The remaining 80 per cent you use to live and to

clear debts. If you have a high level of debt, you may decide to allocate your savings towards clearing debts. Either way, I suggest that you establish the habit of putting some money away for growth in order to change your self image. If you never have any money left over it is hard to perceive yourself as being wealthy. There is nothing like having money at your fingertips, particularly if for most of your life you have never had any. If you are worried that you will be tempted to dip into these savings, enquire about accounts that will prevent you from doing this. Once you can see your savings grow, you will be motivated to move on to the next level.

Make a point of always carrying cash with you. I recommend that you carry $100 in your wallet or purse at all times. It makes you feel prosperous and you will get used to having money.

Before I explain the fundamentals of financial literacy I would like to ask you to suspend all doubt. By this I mean the doubts that many people have about their ability to understand financial matters. Some say, *but I am no good with figures* and because it all seems too hard, they seek advice from advisers who are sometimes more interested in their own commission cheque than in making you rich. I am not saying that all advisers are like that, but the buck stops with you. You cannot make informed decisions if you don't understand the basics of making money.

Assets and liabilities

I am sure you understand that an asset is something you own and a liability is something you owe. Most people would class their house as an asset and their credit card debts as a liability. Am I right?

However, all assets and liabilities are not always as clearcut as they may seem. Robert Kiyosaki[4] has the best explanation I have seen to describe an asset and a liability. Robert says, "An asset is something that

Wealth tip:

Paying your mortgage weekly instead of monthly can save you thousands.

puts money in your pocket. A liability is something that takes money out of your pocket. An asset is something that will feed me while a liability is something that will eat me." Now to me that really sums up what assets and liabilities are all about.

Traditional financial planning classifies houses and cars as assets - but houses and cars take money out of your pocket. Using this interpretation your house and car changes from an asset to a liability.

Wealth tip:
Joint investments automatically revert to the surviving partner. If you want to leave your share to another party invest as tenants-in-common.

The object of investing is to place your money into assets that will provide you with an ongoing and increasing income. A bank deposit will provide you with an income, usually a very poor one but that is not the type of investment I am talking about. Investments such as property, shares and even bonds provide you with an income as well as capital growth. Capital growth simply means that your capital grows in value. This is the way to create real wealth. I love property. I see property as the cornerstone of any investment portfolio. It is good to hold long-term and easy to borrow against. Banks love property. I also have a substantial share portfolio. Traditionally, shares, property and bonds show strong growth at different times in the economic cycle.

By investing in each of the three major investment vehicles, at the appropriate time, you can maximise your returns. You can achieve the types of returns mentioned earlier which can turn your child into a billionaire baby.

Leveraging

One of the major advantages to purchasing property is that you can leverage your investment. Leveraging simply means that you use a small amount of capital to hold a much larger value asset. It means using other people's money.

If you have $20,000 and you invest in an interest bearing investment, only then you receive interest on $20,000. At five per cent interest your investment would grow by $1,000 a year.

On the other hand let's assume you invest $20,000 and borrow $80,000 to buy a property worth $100,000. You would get growth on $100,000. At 10 per cent per annum your investment would grow by $10,000 a year, plus you get the income from the rent. That is the power of leveraging.

The advantages of using leveraging are multiple. Firstly, you usually receive income which helps to pay the costs of the money you borrow. In the case of property investment the rent you receive from your tenants will help pay off the mortgage. Secondly, all of the costs associated with your borrowing, the interest on the loan as well as the purchasing costs are tax deductible. There are further tax deductions to be gained from the costs associated with property such as rates, insurances, agents' fees, inspection costs and depreciation. Depreciation is the allowance that you receive for wear and tear on internal fittings and in some cases the building. These can add up to considerable savings.

Leveraging though does not only apply to property investments, you can leverage an investment in shares

Wealth tip:
One man saved the loose coins from his pocket each day. In 10 years he accumulated $26,000.

as well. Leveraging will multiply your profits as your assets grow, however, in a downturn, leveraging will also increase your losses.

A margin call is made when you have insufficient security in your share portfolio for the lender. If a lender's rules are that they will lend you up to 70 per cent of valuation and the value of your share portfolio falls so that the security drops to 50 per cent, you will have a margin call. That is, you will have to make up the difference. You will get 24 hours notice of a margin call and if you don't come up with the cash or other security, the lender will sell sufficient shares to cover your margin call. However, they make the choice as to which shares they are going to sell, not you.

Why shares?

Often people feel more comfortable about the idea of investing in real estate rather than shares. The reason is that shares are perceived as being more volatile and less tangible. Over a ten year period, shares are likely to increase in value at a similar rate to property. For 10 out of the last 12 decades, shares have actually outperformed real estate.

Wealth tip:
When everyone you know from the man in the street to your fellow workers are talking about investing in property or shares, you usually know the market is close to its peak.

Share prices are reported in the daily newspaper so an investor can always determine the value of their investment. The real value of real estate is only determined when the property is actually sold. Share prices will appear to be relatively stable for long periods and then the value can increase dramatically within a short period. Shares can produce meteoric rises and spectacular falls. A downturn in the sharemarket receives more publicity than a rising market, hence the perception that shares are risky.

An advantage to shares is that you can invest smaller amounts than you can in real estate. If you need money quickly you can usually sell shares just as quickly. Shares offer greater flexibility and if you seek professional advice to assess your individual situation before embarking on this course, they can offer a great return.

Blue chip shares are known for their ability to make profits in good times or bad. Often the dividends paid on blue chip shares are low because of the strong asset backing they provide. Usually blue chip shares will form part of the top 200 companies listed on the Stock Exchange.

Negative gearing

Borrowing to invest is called gearing. When the tax deductible costs of the loan exceed the income earned, it is called negative gearing. That loss therefore can be deducted from your other income, including your wage and therefore can substantially reduce your tax. But remember negative gearing costs you money.

Carol thinks negative gearing is the best thing since sliced bread. In her mid-twenties she decided to stay at home with her parents for a few more years in order to secure a sound financial future for herself. Firstly she saved a deposit and bought her first property. The rent from this plus all the other tax deductions that Carol is entitled to means that the property costs Carol $50 a week. She thinks, and I agree, this is a far better investment for her than saving $50 a week into a bank account. Carol bought her first property three years ago and already it has gone up $60,000 in value.

Carol works as a secretary. When she adds the rent from her property to her wage she has an annual income of $70,000. She is paying tax on considerably less than that amount because she has many items she can write off as tax deductions. Carol plans to buy another two properties and wait until the rent covers the repayments before moving into the first property in two year's time.

The day will come when the rent from Carol's properties will exceed the cost. When this happens this

Wealth tip:
The wisest financial decision you will ever make is to buy your own home and pay it off as quickly as possible.

property will no longer be negatively geared. To avoid additional tax, many people buy more property. By this time the original properties have usually risen in value and you can borrow against these for a deposit to purchase more properties, thereby minimising your tax. This is a strategy many people use to build wealth.

Another couple, Jerry and Pam, who did my *Super Secrets to Wealth* course, told me of their success. In their early fifties they had managed to nearly pay out their home but they had not accumulated any other assets. They decided to use the equity in their home to fund the purchase of some investment properties (equity is your share of the property value after you deduct what is owing on the mortgage). They borrowed $60,000 against their home and purchased two other properties. The interest on all of the money they borrowed to purchase these properties is tax deductible. Because the properties are negatively geared they will have to contribute around $100 a week, but they have calculated that in comparison to paying that same amount into a superannuation fund they would be much better off. Jerry and Pam have structured their plan so that all loans on these properties will be paid off by the time Jerry retires.

Be wary of interest-only loans even if using the money to buy investment property. When you depend on interest-only loans you are counting on inflation being high. What if it is not? Most people who recommend interest-only loans are people with a vested interest, like investment property salesmen who know that you can borrow more on interest-only. I like to own my properties so I always opt for principal and interest loans.

Wealth tip:
Think up strategies in advance to put in place when you feel tempted to fall back on old habits.

It is worth spending a few dollars to get professional advice on your tax planning at the outset. How you set up your plan initially can make a difference of thousands of dollars to you in legitimate tax savings.

I could write a whole book on this one subject, in

fact my *Super Secrets to Wealth* is a programme about wealth building strategies. At this time I have only touched on the basics of leveraging and negative gearing to give you an idea of just how easy it can be.

Protecting your assets

Insurances are an essential part of your financial plan. You need to insure your income, your assets, your life and possibly your health. I am still undecided as to the value of health insurance. It really depends on your state of health and how you look after yourself. In my family, we all take care of ourselves and health problems are minimal so I have opted to invest the money that we would normally pay into a health fund. I know that should a crisis occur we can easily draw on our investments to pay the extra expenses. This way we save considerably, but it really is a personal decision. By making this choice we have decided to self insure. We consider this to be a manageable risk for us.

If you have a mortgage or family to protect then life cover is vital. Actually life cover is rather an inappropriate name because it only pays out in the event of your death. However, there are young people who have no debts and no dependants to protect, who are paying for death cover. In these cases it is really important to reassess whether this is an essential requirement in your financial plan.

Nowadays you can also buy insurance that will pay you a lump sum if you have a heart attack, develop cancer or any number of specified major life-threatening illnesses. The advantage of this type of insurance is that you receive a lump sum to assist you through the recovery period. One man had a heart attack and received a payout of $200,000. This greatly assisted his recovery as he did not have to worry about the financial security of his family.

Wealth tip: *Insure what you cannot live without.*

Income insurance is also necessary until you reach

a point where you can live from your assets. In the building phase, your financial plan would suffer a serious if not terminal set back if you were off work for any lengthy period of time. The cost of this can be minimised by choosing an extended waiting period. By that I mean that if you know you would receive sick pay and holiday pay from your employer for a lengthy period then you could extend the waiting period before you would receive benefits from the insurance company. This would considerably reduce the cost of your premiums.

Income insurance is one where you particularly need to shop around because of the vast difference in premiums for men and women from company to company. Don't assume that one company will be right for both of you. It would be rare if they were. Low premiums are important, but as with anything in life, make sure of what you get for your money. Cheap insurance is not a good investment if when the time comes to claim, you find out that you are not insured for the value you thought.

Income insurance is tax deductible and it is one of the most commonly missed tax claims in preparing tax returns. Some life insurance, if it is set up as key man insurance, can be tax deductible but it is best to check your individual situation first.

As a rule of thumb, I think it is important to have sufficient insurance to pay out all your liabilities in the case of death, prolonged illness or disability. That way, your dependants can enjoy the income from your assets without the worry of handling the debts. You should also add on an extra amount to cover funeral expenses, legal fees, probate and reasonable living expenses for 12 months or so depending upon the size of your asset base.

Wealth tip:
Open a wealth account and use it to build a base for future investments.

Another area of asset protection to consider is how your assets will be protected from litigation and other claims. We live in a litigious society and therefore you need to assess the potential threats to your assets. The rich hide much of their wealth using vehicles such as corporations and trusts to protect their assets from creditors. When someone sues a wealthy individual they are often met with layers of legal protection. Often wealthy people own nothing in their own name. The poor and middle class try to own everything and often lose it to the Government or creditors.

You need to seek appropriate advice on how to best protect your assets from potential claimants.

Make a will

Your will may be the single most important document you create for your children and/or loved ones. Not only does a will outline what happens to your financial assets and designate an executor, it also lays out what you want to happen with your children until they are old enough to be on their own. Major challenges can occur for children if they suddenly lose their parents. Wills cover not only financial matters but who should care for your children and how.

It is very important to discuss your will with your children, even if only to assure them they will be taken care of if something should happen to you and your spouse. The overriding thought that you want to convey is that you have planned for your children to be cared for emotionally and financially by someone. I would emphasise that this plan will probably not be needed until you are quite old and your children are grown up. It is there however, to protect your children in case of an emergency.

Teenage children should know where your will is located. They should also understand their responsibilities if there are younger children.

I also recommend that your teenage children be told about your financial arrangements concerning investments and trust accounts. They need to know

Wealth tip:
Keep 3 months living expenses readily available

where documents are kept, even if they don't know the specifics.

Taxation

Be happy to pay tax. I can imagine you throwing up your hands in horror! I am not advocating you pay more than you have to but there are many ways to legitimately minimise tax. I recommend that you learn as much as you can so you can organise your affairs as effectively as possible. Pay what you legally have to and be grateful that you live in a country where you have so many of the good things in life. Understand that our country is run on the taxes we pay and pay what you need to, happily.

Most common taxation mistakes

Self-assessment means that the Taxation Department puts the onus on you to get your tax return right. If you are audited you have to be able to substantiate your claims and explain any undeclared income. Listed below are some of the most common mistakes and tax claims that are overlooked.

Interest on bank accounts and other financial institutions is commonly overlooked and should be added to your taxable income. The Taxation Department has a system whereby it can check on the interest paid by financial institutions, so make sure you include all interest.

Included in this are dividends paid on shares. Even if you reinvest the dividend and don't actually see the cash, tax is still payable and it must be declared. In the case of dividend imputation a common mistake is to assume that because the company paid tax that you don't have to declare it. You need to declare the gross dividend received and you are entitled to deduct the imputation credit.

There may come a time when your income is higher one year than another, possibly because you have sold an asset and have to pay capital gains tax. There are ways to legitimately reduce your tax bill. One way is to invest in an income producing investment such as term deposits where the interest is paid on 1 July. Or, if you have an investment that is negatively geared you could pre-pay your interest component in advance. You need to seek appropriate professional advice in this area.

FID charges are commonly overlooked as a tax deduction. These fees are charged on your bank account and can be claimed as business or investment expenses, or if your salary is paid into a bank account. They cannot be claimed as your personal expenses.

Income splitting. You can save tax by holding investments in joint names, or better still placing them in the lowest income earner's name. Tax can be minimised considerably using this method.

Depreciation. If you own an investment property you may be able to depreciate fittings, carpets, fixtures and the building in some cases. These savings can amount to thousands of dollars and it is worth having your claims checked by a good accountant to ensure

Wealth tip:
Value every dollar.
Treat it as a
money-seed.

that you are maximising your investment return.

Work related expenses. You can claim up to $300 a year without receipts but this is not a licence to just make a false claim. All claims need to be substantiated. Once your claims exceed $300 receipts are needed for everything.

Capital expenditure. Many people race out and buy equipment in the case of business owners, or fittings in the case of property owners, prior to the 30 June each year in order to claim a tax deduction in that financial year. However, all expenditure over $300 needs to be depreciated for business. If you are a property owner you can only claim the full amount of the expenditure if you spend money on maintenance. If you improve the property or incur larger expenses such as new carpet, you will need to depreciate this expense over a few years.

Travel between workplaces. If you have a second job then you can claim the cost of travelling from one job to another.

Land Tax. If you are a property investor you may be liable for land tax. You can minimise this by proper planning.

These are just a few. I urge you to seek advice from a good accountant to maximise your return if you have investments or earn income other than your salary.

Put your financial affairs in order now

There will always be a reason to procrastinate to avoid having to face your financial situation but it will not go away. You can delegate, get people to help you, pay for advice, but ultimately the responsibility for your financial decisions rests with you.

Wealth tip:
Think of investments in terms of the lifestyle they can provide.

1. Do it now. Decide to be prosperous and commit yourself to putting in the necessary effort. Think positive thoughts, develop a can-do attitude and a prosperous belief system. Visualise your dreams

and focus on what you want. Constantly affirm that you deserve to be prosperous.

2. Develop a wealth accumulation plan and set your goals.

3. Start with an income and expense statement. Know how much comes in and how much goes out.

4. Know how much credit is costing you. If you really want a fright add it up over the year and multiply it for the past five years. That ought to be enough to motivate you to make changes.

5. Reassess your spending. Check how you can minimise your outgoings so that there is more to put towards your wealth building account. Save first and spend what is left.

6. Reassess your insurances. Do you have enough protection? Are you paying the best rates? Do you have excessive cover?

7. Are you paying too much tax? If you are not sure it is worth paying for advice. Incidentally if you forgot to claim some items over the last few years you can lodge an amended claim.

8. Shop around for mortgage rates.

9. If you are just getting started and you don't own a home yet make buying a home your first priority. Save at least 20 per cent of your income and more if it is possible. Your home can later be used to create even greater wealth.

10. Take time to gain knowledge. The more you read and the more courses you take, the greater your understanding of the financial system will be. Observe wealthy people. Spend time around someone who is doing well. Study their behaviours and beliefs and let these rub off on you.

Wealth tip:
Never go to the automatic teller machine more than once a week.

11. Value your money. Treat it like you would your best friend. You will reap the rewards.

12. Enjoy it. Money is to be enjoyed. If occasions arise when you have to spend then do so wholeheartedly. If you follow all the above steps you will have nothing to worry about.

In Summary

1. Give away 10 per cent of all you earn. Save 10 per cent of all you earn.

2. Remember assets feed you while liabilities eat you.

3. Use leveraging to create wealth.

4. Protect your assets.

5. Seeks ways to minimise tax legitimately.

6. Start today

Chapter Twelve

The entrepreneurial age

Most of us spend a great part of our lives working. If life is to be a delight then we need to feel our work is worthwhile.

Mark Victor Hansen

Opportunities are all around you. They did not end with the industrial age. They are not over the next mountain. They are right in front of you.

The industrial age began in Great Britain about 1760. It was a time that brought great changes to the way people worked and lived. Manual techniques of production made way for machines, self-sufficiency made way for employer/employee relationships. I am sure if we had lived back then we would have found that such changes struck fear into the hearts of many people who did not know what the future would hold.

The advancement of technology has brought great changes to our lives and the way people work. Employees are being made redundant not because of a downturn in the economy, but because jobs have been taken over by computers. No longer can we be guaranteed a job and drastic change tends to makes people fearful. All change brings with it opportunity. Robert Kiyosaki[4] says:

Land was wealth 300 years ago. So the person who owned the land owned the wealth. Then, it was factories and production, and America rose to dominance. The industrialist owned the wealth. Today, it is information. And the person who has the most timely information owns the wealth. The problem is, information flies all around the world at the speed of light. The new wealthy cannot be contained by boundaries and borders as land and factories were. The change will be faster and more dramatic. There will be a dramatic increase in the number of new multimillionaires. There also will be those who are left behind.

If you are to continue to grow, you need to advance with the times and become entrepreneurial. One thing is certain, the entrepreneurial age will bring with it increased self-employment. More people will work from home and believe it or not, there will be more opportunities. They will be different opportunities from those you are used to. It is true that our children can no longer be assured of getting a job when they leave school, but that doesn't mean that they can't find better opportunities. There are a lot of pluses to being self-employed. You just need to develop your creativity in order to recognise the multitude of opportunities that are all around you.

A woman advertised a typing business in the businesses for sale column of a major newspaper. One of the callers who responded to the advertisement worked as a public servant.

She said, "Who pays you if there is no work?"

The business owner replied, "No-one. If there is no work you don't get paid, that is what being self-employed is all about."

When you make a real decision, you draw a line, and it's not in the sand but in cement.

Anthony Robbins

The young caller responded, "Well that hardly seems fair".

Surprisingly this belief that someone should pay us whether we work or not, is not as uncommon as one would think. Just because you are alive, educated or uneducated, does not mean that you are entitled to a job. You are responsible for creating your own opportunities.

Anthony Sahade was attending the Sydney Conservatory of Music. He was the leader of the Sydney Youth Orchestra playing the violin. To earn extra money in his final year Anthony approached a local service station and offered to lease a space to wash cars, it wasn't anything flash. They hand washed the cars using buckets and rags, much the same as the boy scouts. He made about a $100 a day.

Anthony was continually looking for ideas to attract more people into the car wash. At one time he placed a scantily-clad mannequin on the premises to attract passing motorists and it worked. The weekend business grew and grew and so did the turnover of the garage. At the end of the day, Anthony found that he had to continually pick up drink cans and wrappers from the area he leased. The turnover of drinks actually quadrupled while Anthony worked there.

The demand for refreshments gave Anthony an idea. When he finished his studies he decided to go into business for himself. Instead of getting his customers to just stand around while their car was being cleaned, he gave them a place to relax, have a cappuccino and something to eat while they read the morning papers. That idea became Crystal Car Wash and Rita's Cafe. In 1996 Crystal Car Wash had a turnover of $5 million and employed 100 workers. They also use 160 kgs of coffee each year.

Recognising opportunities

Some people make money by setting a specific goal and following a set course of action. Sometimes though, we don't know how to achieve our goals but don't let that stop you from doing what you want. Often opportunities occur when we least expect them so it is important to keep an open mind and be flexible.

Enjoy the journey to wherever you want to go.

Faith Popcorn is one of America's foremost trend

forecasters of business trends. Faith foresaw the demand for four-wheel drives, home delivery and the failure of new Coke. She works with some of the world's top companies such as American Express, IBM and Nissan, and she is the author of two books *The Popcorn Report* and *Clicking*. Being a forecaster of trends is not what Faith set out to be. After leaving school Faith did a visual arts course and started working in advertising. She was fired from her first job. After several years working in the advertising industry, Faith was tired of the corporate world and decided to open her own business with her creative partner from the agency, Stuart Pittman. They called their business BrainReserve. Faith says "we didn't have a clue what a 'BrainReserve' would be or could be." I will let Faith tell you the rest in her own words[14]:

Phil Dougherty of the New York Times, called to say that he was intrigued by the names Popcorn and BrainReserve, and wanted to set up an interview. Pandemonium and panic set in. What should we do? What should we say?

I rang up my friends and family, casting about for the way to maximise this tremendous opportunity. My thoughts ran like this: 'If we get a favourable mention in that column, we'd be made." But there were no major success stories to brag about. Since I couldn't impress him by spinning tales of recent triumphs, I decided to describe what we talk about every day at our office. Predictions of what we thought was going to happen and why. It was as simple as that.

BrainReserve was recognised as a futurist marketing company, and I was its fearless leader. After so many scared, friendless, uncomfortable, hard years, I had figured out what I could do that was unique: channelling problems into solutions through a future vision. I'd Clicked into the right combination - out of my cage, out of my rage, into a new age.

Wealth tip:
There are opportunities all around you.

Future Trends

In her books, Faith predicts where opportunities will lie in the future and some of these are listed below.

Controlled escape: Computers will take us on mind-trips to exotic destinations or back in time.

Age of the Brain: Classes on how to use our brains, brain gyms, brain clubs. Anything that enhances our brain such as thinking herbs will be popular.

Time Out: People will want to take a year off from their daily work. Opportunities exist for indulgence planners, destinations, leisure experts.

Beauty as science: With the ageing of the baby boomers opportunities exist in areas that prevent aging, including cosmetics, reconstructive surgery, fitness, better vision.

Composting Industry: Easy ways to compost, recycle and re-use. Opportunities are available for practical bins that work, videos, classes, books, consultancies.

Fast food places for babies.

Dream Architects. A consultancy business helping people make their dreams come true.

Delivery Service. All types of delivery services and home-based shopping businesses will thrive.

What others have done

If you are ever looking for a unique, idea America seems to be the place for doing the unusual. The following ideas come from the book, *Finding Your Perfect Work* by Sarah and Paul Edwards[15]:

- Robin Sherman provides a service called rent-a-mum.

- Marcia Foots has a concierge service in the lobby of three dozen residential and office buildings to help tenants pick up dry cleaning, obtain theatre tickets and take cars for servicing.

- One psychologist does mobile therapy. She picks her clients up in a limo and they have a session on the

Never underestimate yourself.

way to or from work or during their lunch hour.

- Myla Fahn hand paints the bride and grooms likeness onto wedding cake decorations, including their faces and exact replicas of what they wore.

- Architect inventor David Hertz takes rubbish of all kinds, grinds it up and turns it into synecrite, a lightweight concrete from which he makes tiles, tabletops, flooring and so on.

- Rebecca Cole creates miniature gardens inside all types of recyclable containers from old flour bins to old leather satchels.

- Natalie Lederman (at 12) created jewellery from aluminium drink cans.

- Jake Blehm sells killer bugs that help farmers eradicate pesticides.

- Marrion Forrest creates lifelike dolls with faces and clothing done as exact duplicates of children for their grandparents.

- Someone else started up gift baskets for divorcees.

- Two enterprising women, unhappy with the service they were getting from their car dealer, started Fix-A-Car - a referral service for people wanting help in finding a good mechanic.

- A stay-at-home dad started a newsletter for men who choose fatherhood over a career.

Technology brings with it new opportunities. According to Sarah and Paul, 50 of the best home businesses available today were not available 25 years ago

According to the NSW Enterprise Workshop, the key qualities of successful business people are:

Life does not stand still. Either you decide where you are going or you will be dragged along by other people.

Commitment
Optimism
Perseverance
Enthusiasm

Willingness to seek advice
Organisational ability
Responsibility
Confidence

Remember though that all of these qualities can be developed if you have a willingness to grow.

Your opportunities are unlimited

Remember the children's game noughts and crosses? There are nine squares that you usually put a nought or a cross in. If you were to substitute the noughts and crosses with numbers from one through to 9, then switched them around, using different combinations each time, how many different arrangements do you think you could find?[19]

There are actually **362,880** possible combinations. Surprising isn't it?

When we think about what we want from life and how we can achieve it, we usually limit ourself to what we can see, or know. If we can find 362,880 combinations from nine numbers and nine squares, how many opportunities could there be for us that we haven't thought about yet?

Brainstorming

Designing a life takes time and is not something you can usually do in one session. Choosing work that excites you can go beyond what you know or expect at the present time. So, allow yourself to be creative by asking some close friends to join you in a brainstorming session. Even if you already know what you want to do, you can use this exercise to come up with ways to get started.

The object of brainstorming is to pick a topic. Then with a group of people, try to come up with as many ideas about that subject as you can. You may want to nominate one person to write everything down, or you could record your session. The point of this exercise is

Everything starts with an idea.

not to talk, discuss or judge, but to be open-minded to every suggestion no matter how way out it may seem at the time. When you start making judgements, you stop the creative process and your logical left brain takes over. Of course some of the ideas will be garbage and you can weed those out later. At the brainstorming stage, put down anything that comes to mind.

Sarah and Paul Edwards did an exercise on brainstorming for career choices in their book *Finding Your Perfect Work*,[15] to suit someone who likes to work with animals, and we added a few of our own to their list as well.

Vet

Vet nurse

Animal training

Animal training for film/television

Pet minder

Animal grooming service

Pet psychologist

Data base matching service matching animal types to owners

Grief counsellor for people who have lost pets

Animal cemetery

Animal casks/headstones

Animal stuffing

Animal photographer/painter

Manufacture house/clothes/accessories for animals

Make animal cookies

Make home-cooked meals for dogs

Pet register/locating hard to find animals

Pet judge

Breed animals

Start pet shows

Make animal toys

Wealth tip:
When you fulfil your life's purpose, your destiny, you will fulfil your desires.

Write a column on unusual animals

Work as a journalist on an animal show

Be a researcher for an animal show

Publish or write books on animals

When you change your mindset from one of limitation to abundant opportunities, you will find that there are more opportunities available to you today than ever before, and they will continue to grow. Throughout the coming weeks, whenever you feel doubtful, remind yourself constantly that there are infinite possibilities.

I read this short story in Wayne Dyer's book *You'll see it when you believe it*[16].

"Excuse me," said one ocean fish to another, "you are older and more experienced than I, and will probably be able to help me. Tell me: where can I find this thing they call the ocean? I've been searching for it everywhere to no avail."

"The ocean," said the older fish, "is what you are swimming in now."

"Oh, this? But this is only water. What I'm searching for is the ocean," said the young fish, feeling quite disappointed.

Opportunities are all around you. They are not over the next mountain, they are right in front of you but you won't always recognise them until you look for them.

This is the age of the entrepreneur and it is the most thrilling, exciting time of all to be alive.

In Summary

1. Change brings opportunities.

2. You cannot necessarily count on a job any more but you can create your own employment.

3. Develop the qualities of successful people.

4. Look for opportunities in every situation.

Chapter Thirteen

Teach your children about money

Your children are not your children they are the sons and daughters of life's longing for itself.

Kahlil Gibran

Children learn from what we do, not from what we say.

Children are expensive. According to figures from The Australian Institute of Family Studies magazine, a child will cost $204 every week, from the first week of life. These costs fluctuate throughout differing life stages ranging from $167 a week to $243 a week during the teenage years. Allowing for the cost of housing, clothing, medical, dental and education expenses a child can cost you in the vicinity of $200,000 if he goes to private school and university. Not only do you have to meet these costs but all that your children learn about money will come from you.

Most people have preconceived ideas about what they will do when they become parents. And as anyone who has children knows, most of these theories fly out the window when you are faced with the prospect of forcing your will on an often unwilling child. Babies have a mind of their own and it doesn't get any easier as they grow up.

I have known many well-meaning parents who have asked me, *How can I teach my children to save and be good with money?* It's not a matter of one day sitting down and explaining the ins and outs of money management to them. That went out with the talk about the birds and bees. Children learn about money every day by the things you say, your actions, through your struggles, your fights and your achievements.

When our children were younger they would often come home and say, *Why can't we have a new car like…?* and they would mention the family of a friend they played with. There were many things that our children wanted that we had to say "no" to, and each time I would use this as an opportunity to explain to them that we invest our money so that we can have things that are really important to us. I would explain the principles of having your money working for you, rather than you working for it.

The easy money syndrome

One man used to spend constantly on consumer items and most of them were paid for with his credit card. Whenever he went shopping with his children they would say, "Just put it on the plastic Dad." The day came when this man decided to cut up his credit cards and totally change his habits and at the same time he had to re-educate his children. All they knew from a very young age was that if you wanted something, you bought it. They had no history of making choices. They were conditioned that instant gratification was normal. Fortunately, this man became aware of what he was teaching his children by his actions before it was too late.

In changing his habits this man turned his family's entire financial situation around. Whereby once they lived from week to week and always had substantial debts on credit cards, he now chose to use cash. He refinanced his loans. He started saving. Within 12

One of the things that often holds us back in our success is the deliberate attempt we make to hide from the facts when the facts are unpleasant.

Sterling W Sill

months he had saved a considerable amount. He received a substantial pay rise at work. This often happens when you change your money habits because your self image changes and other people unconsciously pick up the energy changes in you. This man was able to demonstrate to his sons, by his actions and his words, that there was a better way to manage money.

The same applies to automatic teller machines. I have heard many children tell their parents to *Just get the money from the machine*. The advancement of technology has given many children the mistaken impression that there is a never-ending supply of money. When my children said this we explained to them that you had to have money in the bank before you could take it out. To have money in the bank you had to earn it first.

Money skills come naturally when they are taught by example

There is an abundance of classes available to teach children a whole range of skills from dancing, swimming, tennis, acting, horseriding, scouts and so on. We think nothing of providing our children with a rich environment of experiences so that they can gain valuable life skills. When it comes to money there is little education provided in the home or school environment. Yet, we expect them to grow up and become responsible with money. When you think about it, it doesn't make sense.

We learn by repetition and practise. The same applies to smart money skills. Everyday experiences provide us with an abundance of opportunities to teach our children about money.

When I was in the direct-selling business I got into the habit of driving up to the 'Change Given' window on a tollway and asking for a receipt. I still do this today, and I explain to my children that because I am going to see a client, I can claim the toll as a tax

Going to the experts is expensive. But it is infinitely cheaper than experience.

Robert Allen

deduction. My children learnt that you need to keep records in order to substantiate deductions and minimise tax. They have become used to asking for receipts whenever they buy something.

From around the age of six or seven our children have been paid pocket money each week - but only for jobs that they do. If they don't work, they don't get paid, just like in the real world. We have a roster in our kitchen which details before school jobs and after school jobs. There are also extra jobs that anyone of the children can do if they wish to earn extra money. This could be sweeping out the garage, washing the car, mowing the lawns. All of these jobs have set amounts of pay attached to them. If any of my children do this extra work, then they have to give me an invoice. I pay immediately once I receive an invoice, but they don't get paid if they don't produce an invoice. In business I have seen so many people lose money simply because they have not learnt the simple skill of preparing an invoice for work done. I teach my children about business.

When we go on holidays, each child is given a set amount of money and they have to account for it. For instance on our last holiday at the Gold Coast we paid the entrance fee into Dreamworld. Once inside, if our children wanted anything extra they had to pay for it. We don't tell them what to buy, we give them free choice. They are also aware that once the money runs out there is no more.

When you lurch from one financial crisis to another you will continue to get more of the same. Change the way you think and act.

When shopping with your children talk about the reasons why you buy. Point out that the magazine and lolly rack are located near the cash register so that you will impulse buy.

Be aware that the buying decisions you make teaches your children about values. For instance, do you buy locally made products? Do you choose environmentally friendly products? Do you think about health when shopping by buying low fat, low salt, low sugar products? Do you look for generic brands? What do you do if you receive more change than is due to you?

We are all bombarded with advertising every day. We discuss advertisements and encourage our children to look beyond the glossy image. We teach our children to recognise sales strategies so that they will become informed consumers.

I encourage my children to write out cheques themselves when we have to pay for something on their behalf. It takes longer but they are learning a vital skill, including filling in the cheque butt.

My son Michael has approached me on a number of occasions with money making ideas. I always commend him on his ideas and discuss them with him in depth. I have shown him how to carry out market research and how to assess what resources he will need to implement his ideas. He rings up suppliers himself. He has several folders containing research information on various projects. Not only is he gaining valuable skills, his self confidence has grown as well.

My son recently went through this exercise to find the best value for some scuba diving gear he wanted. He ordered from a supplier located 300 kms away from our home and the supplier offered to deliver freight free. He also obtained a discount.

Educate your children

My parents always said, "Whatever you put in your mind no-one can take from you." What is in your mind is more important than any other thing. Consequently, we are happy to spend on any type of education. We really value education and not only the academic type. We consider that the broader a field of life experiences our children have, the more skilled they will be at making choices.

Carina, my eldest daughter, did a Discovery course

When you know what is important to you, making decisions comes easily.

at age 13. This boosted her self esteem enormously. She has also done Bob Proctor's Born Rich course and a creative writing course at Charles Sturt University.

On holidays in Cairns one year Carina and Michael both wanted to learn scuba diving. Michael loved it and continued lessons and is now a qualified scuba diver. Carina decided that it wasn't something that she wanted to pursue. I constantly say to them try it, check it out and then decide if you want to continue with it.

All of our children are strongly encouraged to do higher education, but we also don't try to live their life for them. My son is extremely clever but has no interest in the business world. He likes working with his hands and wants to be a builder. He wants to get an apprenticeship and become a tradesman.

Teach your children to save and invest

Our children have to save half of all they earn in a bank account. When these savings accumulate to a reasonable sum I take the money and invest it for them. These investments are held under a family trust, partly for tax planning but mostly because I want to teach my children to keep their assets together. All of our children own shares and they own a share of a property as well. Although they don't have access to the capital they have access to the income from their investments and there have been times when this has been able to give them wonderful opportunities.

At the age of 15 Carina went to Germany and lived there for three months with relatives. She paid for this trip with income from her investments. She also had a credit card that she could use for emergencies. When Carina returned home after three months, she still had money left over. Carina has a wealth mentality and is going to be very rich one day.

Actions speak louder than words

On the other hand my other two children Michael and Stephanie both like to spend money before they earn it and they may have to learn the hard way. All children are individuals and some are naturally thrifty while others need more encouragement.

Because we talk about money at the dinner table, our children are aware of many of the companies we hold shares in. They also help to clean up and maintain some of our rental properties from time to time. It is part of the teaching process and we want them to understand what is involved in managing investments.

Treat your children the way you want them to be

When children make mistakes it is not uncommon to criticise them and tell them what they have done wrong. We often have preconceived ideas about our children, about their intelligence, their ability to accept responsibility, to make friends and so on. And, we act on these preconceived ideas every day.

When a child spends all they earn, a natural reaction is to lecture them about the responsibilities of handling money. The way we treat our children is the way they will be.

An alternative way to treat them is to act as if they were already the responsible child that you want them to be. It takes patience and effort at first, particularly if you don't see any immediate results, but children and adults alike will usually live up, or down, to our expectations.

Goethe said, "Treat a man as he is and he will remain as he is, treat a man as he can and should be and he will become what he can and should be."

Create a different environment for your children. See the good in them. See all that they can be and should be, and watch them blossom.

Motivate your children

I read this story in the Sydney Morning Herald Money section[17]. Peter Thornhill who is a general

It's not about how much you make. It's about how much of it you get to keep and how hard you make it work for you. That's Financial Intelligence.

Robert Kiyosaki

manager for MLC Superannuation and Investments told of how he motivates his sons. When each of his boys turned 13 he gave them a share trust investment with a few thousand dollars. The details of these investments were placed in their computer and each quarter when dividends were declared they would update their records. This way the boys had an idea of how the market worked.

When his 20 year old son was at university, he was saving $50 a week from a part-time job. Peter explained that if he continued to save this amount at 12 per cent he would have $1.4 million in 35 years. Peter said, "It took him five seconds to decide he wanted to save $100 a week."

We have fostered in our children a spirit of independence and respect for money, and more importantly, we have taught them to value themselves and to dream. Our children dream big dreams. Teach your children they can have what they want and then show them how by doing it for yourself. It will be one of the greatest gifts you can give them.

In Summary

1. Children learn from what you do, not what you say.

2. Teach your children that money has to be earned.

3. Use everyday experiences to teach your children about money management.

4. Treat your children as if they already are the way you want them to be.

5. Motivate your children by showing them how to make money easily.

6. Encourage your children to dream big dreams.

Bite off more than you can chew, then chew like crazy.

Crocodile Dundee

Chapter Fourteen

What the rich do

When it comes to making money the only skill most people have is to work hard.

Robert Kiyosaki

The rich know that the only way to real wealth is to have your money working for you.

If you are looking for a path that can take you to the next level of prosperity then you need to know about money skills. Having known many prosperous people over my lifetime, I have observed that there are seven essential money skills that they share and these are:

1. They value it
2. They make it
3. They manage it
4. They save it
5. They invest it
6. They shield it
7. They share it

The rich value money

In other words they do not squander it and they treat money and possessions with respect. Rich people know that money is an asset that can be used to create more wealth and in turn to provide greater freedom. They may be generous at times and they may allow themselves all the luxuries they choose, but that does not mean they squander their money.

I remember once hearing Robert Kiyosaki talking about a time when he was collecting rent from tenants in one of his apartment buildings. He was amazed to find how many of them had a big screen TV, the latest CD player, CDs and all the latest consumer toys available. His comment at the time was that he chose to buy apartment blocks instead, which in turn would provide him with an income stream. That phase for Robert was only temporary and I am sure that now he could buy himself all the big screen TVs he desires. The point is that he valued money enough to make it work for him.

Not all rich people value money and those who don't usually don't stay rich for long. There are stories galore of entrepreneurs who made it big, only to lose it all just as quickly. These are usually the ones who spend it all on big consumer toys. Not that many years ago there was one well known entrepreneur who bought his wife a helicopter for her birthday. They had matching luxury cars. Every time you opened the paper there was an article about this couple and their latest flamboyance. Not surprisingly, he lost all his money and eventually went bankrupt.

There are many rich people that are not obviously rich. They don't flash their wealth about, or brag about it. They just quietly go about their business, increasing their asset base and enjoying their riches in the process. Often they quietly share it with others. They are the truly wealthy.

I encourage you to value each and every dollar that flows into your life, because you can achieve financial freedom on just one dollar a day. Use it or lose as the *Never invest more* Bible says. Prosperous people don't think that a dollar *than you are* is just a dollar. They imagine it as a seed. A money *prepared to lose.* seed that has the power to grow into a huge money tree supplying fruit to fulfil every one of their dreams.

Every time you waste one of those little gold coins, you are throwing away a money seed. That simple money seed contains the power to bless you and countless future generations. If you start now a wealthy future awaits you. Let nothing divert you from your task. Remember, it all starts with a single dollar. Value it!

The rich make money

Some earn it doing work that they love. Others make their money from looking after their investments. The smartest ones do both.

There are two ways to make money. You can go to work and exchange your time and skills for money or, you can put your money out to work for you.

When you work for someone else your work is temporary. You may think you have job security but in our current times no-one can be assured of a job forever. Not everyone wants to be self-employed and you don't have to be to build strong income-producing asset base. If you do want to be self-employed don't be discouraged by temporary setbacks.

I once heard about a study that was done on a group of people who had made a million dollars before the age of 30. The group were asked how many businesses they had been involved in before they became millionaires. The average number was 18. The one trait they all shared was tenacity and patience. Those qualities will help you achieve what you want. It is not uncommon for people in business to lose money during the first few years.

A number of people in business were asked why they ventured out on their own and these were the six top motivators:

To pursue a passion
To be financially independent
To escape from the rat race

Focus on the things you want, not the things you don't want.

To be free to be more creative
To have greater freedom
To be rich.

The 10 per cent factor

If you are a man who stands six feet tall and you add 10 per cent you become a giant. If you subtract 10 per cent you become short. Dramatic changes can occur when you add or subtract 10 per cent to your efforts, your perseverance and your enthusiasm.

Imagine an employee who decides to work 10 per cent harder, 10 per cent longer and aspires 10 per cent higher. Don't you think that employee would stand out from the crowd?

Or a business owner who decides to give 10 per cent more value, 10 per cent better service and 10 per cent more to his staff. Would this person's business not grow?

Add to this 10 per cent more faith. 10 per cent more energy. 10 per cent more joy.

Give all you've got then give 10 per cent more and watch what happens. This is the foundation of great leadership.

Most people know the old expression about ostriches burying their head in the sand whenever they are afraid. This is not true and seems to be a trait bestowed on them by humans. But humans act this way often by denying the facts that are right in front of them.

Wealth tip:
Loan repayments on all debts including mortgage, credit cards etc. should come to no more than 30 per cent of your gross income.

The rich manage their money

Money, like time, needs to be managed or it will disappear. The rich know the value of managing their money.

Two men left school 40 years ago. They both started work at the same time, one as a postman, the other in a bank. The first man loved his job and never progressed beyond the level of a postman. He valued money and managed it carefully. He saved and invested. When he retires in a few years time this man's investment portfolio will be worth around $3 million dollars. All on a postman's salary.

The other man worked in the bank for a few years then left and went to work in private industry. He ended up as a general manager. However, he always felt that he needed to live up to an image. Most of his money went into upholding this image. When he retires in a few years time he will have his superannuation payout which will be around $300,000 and his family home.

To summarise what good money managers do:

1. They plan their needs and procrastinate their wants.

2. They always shop for value.

3. They ask for and expect a discount.

4. They obtain a receipt.

5. They claim a tax deduction if their purchases qualify.

6. They balance their accounts, whether it is cash, cheque or credit card.

7. They file their receipts and other documents for easy reference.

The rich save their money

The rich know that small amounts can grow to substantial sums. They build a financial reserve that will cover them during a downturn and will support them later on. They may be bold but they do not trust to luck.

Remember the statistics I quoted in the first chapter how only a handful achieve financial independence

Wealth tip:
If fixed rates on mortgages are offered for a long term you can just about guarantee that the lending institution expects interest rates to go down.

by retirement? Those figures could be interpreted as follows:

3 per cent work, manage and plan
10 per cent work and manage
87 per cent work

It is not that 87 per cent are not good workers. The grim reality is that unless you do as the rich do, that is work, manage and plan, chances are you will become just another statistic.

The first rule of saving is the sooner you start the more you will have. Habits are established by starting. Talking about what you are going to do one day will get you nowhere. Even if you are in debt, establish the habit of saving even small amounts from your pay regularly. I mentioned the power of compound interest. Delaying the commencement of your financial plan will cost you a lot more than just weekly savings.

Let's assume you decided to save $50 a week. If you saved this amount and it earned 10 per cent interest for 30 years you would accumulate around $445,829. Delay saving for just one year and you will accumulate $402,927. A difference of $35,902 from just $2,600 in savings. And for every year that you delay, the gap widens. Start this week. Start right now!

The rich invest their money at attractive rates of return

Wealth tip:
Don't
automatically
place all
investments in
joint names. You
could pay more
tax than is
necessary.

They use their money and assets to make them grow. You can invest in your own education, a business, property, shares or a range of investments. Where you invest your money will have an enormous impact on how much it grows.

Choice magazine states that in one year alone, Australians will miss out on $4 billion in interest by leaving their money in a basic transaction account with banks[18].

Julie started saving at 17. In one year she managed

to save $1,200 only to discover that her bank paid her 0.25 per cent interest on her savings. Imagine just a quarter of one per cent! You can imagine how long it would take Julie to make any money on her savings at that rate.

A percentage point or two may not seem to make much difference in the short term but it can add up to enormous amounts over time. Just imagine if Julie continued saving for the next 40 years. If her investments earned 2 per cent, which is the most basic return that savings accounts pay at the moment, her savings would grow to $73,144. If Julie decided to move these savings to a term deposit and earn say 5 per cent, then over 40 years her savings would grow to $148,252. If Julie invested her money and averaged 12 per cent return over the same time frame, then she would accumulate $970,000.

Julie could earn $73,000 or $970,000 from her savings just by learning a little about investments. It pays big dollars to understand the money game and any money you spend in gaining this knowledge can be a valuable investment.

What you do with your money is important

Equally as important as the return on an investment is where you place your money. Most of us would like to think our money is doing some good. Property is always a good investment because it provides housing for others. In Australia six per cent of the population houses one-third of the population. These statistics not only confirm the demand and viability of property but they are a good indicator as to its long term prospects.

Investing in managed funds has become a popular vehicle in recent years. It is interesting to note that some ethical funds have been generating very healthy returns over recent years. However, the word ethical has broad connotations and you should take care by

Invest in companies that are environmentally responsible.

reading the prospectus as to what it implies.

According to Choice magazine[18] the top 10 issues for investors were:

Environmental protection
Sustainable land use
Forest logging/woodchipping
Reafforestation
Energy/resource use efficiency
Militarism and armaments
Repressive regimes
Fair labour/work practices
Uranium mining
Racism/discrimination

Money talks and your savings have the power to contribute to a safer, healthier, more abundant world for everyone.

The rich shield their assets

They protect what they have by having adequate insurance cover and protecting themselves against risk. They also learn how to structure their affairs to minimise taxes.

If you were to set out on a long holiday with your family by car think about what you would do. Most people would have the car checked for roadworthiness. Then they would fill their petrol tank, check their oil and tyres, including the spare tyre. If you were going to be travelling through isolated country you would take along petrol, water and some basic tools. In other words you would do all that you could to minimise risk to ensure that you all have a safe and happy holiday. Many do all this for a holiday but when it comes to safeguarding their financial future and asset base they often trust to luck.

Many of life's failures are people who did not realise how close they were to success when they gave up.

Thomas Edison

Adequate insurance is what will ensure your peace of mind and financial security.

The rich also take advantage of tax structures and

as I mentioned earlier it is a well-known fact that the rich often pay less tax. That is not because they are dishonest but because they know how to work the system. Many legitimate deductions will enable you to reduce your tax while you are building an asset base. In effect the Government, via lower taxes, is making a contribution to your savings.

For every legitimate tax minimisation scheme, there are just as many schemes whereby you may appear to save money but the reality is that you lose control. According to the press reports that I have read, the late Michael Hutchence was worth around $40 million when he tragically committed suicide. At that level of wealth, tax minimisation is essential. From reports I read, Michael appeared to have all his money tied up in companies and trusts to the point where he did not actually own anything himself. He also lost control of his own assets. The end result is that his de facto wife and child may not receive anything from his estate.

I am not against companies and trusts, just the opposite. Just take care that you have control and your assets are protected and will go to the beneficiaries of your choice in the event of your death.

On the subject of tax minimisation I strongly suggest that you set it up legitimately. Tax minimisation is tax avoidance not tax evasion. Tax evasion is illegal and carries heavy penalties.

A friend told me of a couple that sought advice on a financial matter from her. This couple told her that they were using false names and they would not give an address or phone number for fear of the repercussions. They said that over the years they had a very successful retail business and they had been advised to take cash from it and not declare it. Over time the cash takings amounted to hundreds of thousands of dollars. Each time they went overseas on holidays they

I am not evading tax in any way, shape or form. Of course, I am minimising my tax. Anybody in this country who does not minimise his tax wants his head read. I can tell you as a government that you are not spending it so well that we should be donating extra.

Kerry Packer

took cash out of the country and placed it in accounts in foreign lands.

Now they were retired and wanted to enjoy the fruits of their labour but they were unable to do this. They had been investigated by the Taxation Department who went over their affairs with a fine tooth comb. They suspected that someone had dobbed them in. They were so afraid of being found out that they lived a very modest lifestyle with very modest possessions in order not to draw attention to themselves.

Whenever they wanted to holiday overseas they would have garage sales and various other public events to raise money. This was to divert suspicion from themselves and to prove they raised the money legitimately if they were ever audited by the Taxation Department.

They consulted my friend to discover how they could bring the money back into the country without arousing suspicion. My friend couldn't help them.

This couple had accumulated millions of dollars yet could not even enjoy them. If they had paid for some good advice, learnt more about their options, and done their tax planning properly in the first place this situation would never have arisen.

The rich pay taxes, they just use every legitimate opportunity to minimise them.

The rich share their wealth

Money is merely a tool with which we enrich our own lives and the lives of others. The rule of giving 10 per cent of your income away is not new and I can personally vouch that the more you give, the more you receive.

Trust is putting your beliefs into action.

Most people are good hearted and the reason that they don't give is because they don't believe that there will be enough to go around. Rich people walk their talk. They know that giving not only benefits others, it eliminates fear. Fear is one of the major barriers to wealth accumulation. Giving freely for its own sake will reap its own rewards. I believe that what we sow, we reap.

Sharing your money really is a skill. The Rockefellers believed that giving money away was essential to wealth. I encourage you to establish a legacy that will outlive you. Plant trees that others will pick the fruit from. The more you have the more you can share. Sometimes we hold ourselves back from having all that we want because we don't want to embarrass others, or leave them behind. You will do more for your fellow man by having all that your heart desires, then sharing how to do this with him. Bring your fellow man up to your level. You don't help him by staying down there with him.

In Summary

1. The rich value money.

2. The rich know how to make money.

3. The rich manage their money.

4. The rich save their money.

5. The rich invest their money.

6. The rich shield their money.

7. The rich share their good fortune with others.

Here's a two-step formula for handling stress.

Step 1: Don't sweat the small stuff.

Step 2: Remember, it's all small stuff.

Anthony Robbins

Chapter Fifteen

Being rich and happy

Spread love everywhere you go: first of all in your own house. Give love to your children, your wife or husband, to a next door neighbour...Let no one ever come to you without leaving better and happier. Be the living expression of God's kindness; kindness in your face, kindness in your eyes, kindness in your smile, kindness in your warm greeting.

Mother Teresa

There are three facets to being rich and happy and they are being, doing and having.

Being represents the person that you want to be. In other words developing the character, values and ethics of your highest ideals. Are you the person that you want to be? Ask yourself these questions:

Would I like to have myself for a spouse?
Would I like to have me for a parent?
Would I like to have me for a boss?
Would I like to have me for a friend?

If you can answer 'yes' to all those questions then you are well on the way to being the person that you want to be. Putting off being the person that you want to be or living the life you want until you succeed, or making it to the next rung on the ladder, just doesn't work. There is only today and while we plan for tomorrow, we do the best we can with who we are and what we have today.

Wayne Dyer says that you do not change something by focusing on what is wrong with you. If you focus on what is lacking, that is what you will attract. You become the person you want to be by doing. You simply fill yourself up with more of what you want and the unwanted aspects of your character will just fade away. If you want to be more loving forget about what you do now, just practise being more loving.

Take time to be the person that you want to be. If you would like to be kinder, do it now. If you would like to be more generous, do it now. If you would like to be more loving, do it now. If you want to take more time for relaxation, do it now. If you want to learn to climb mountains or paint, do it now. If you want to be more considerate of others, do it now. If you want to tell someone you love them, do it now.

I read this story on random acts of kindness in Chicken Soup for the Soul[5] and it brought home to me the simple acts that we can do everyday to make the world a better place.

Let others lead small lives, but not you. Let others argue over small things, but not you. Let others cry over small hurts, but not you. Let others leave their future in someone else's hands, but not you.

Jim Rohn

On a crisp winter day a woman was driving over the San Francisco Bay bridge, her car full of Christmas presents. She pulled up to the toll gate and said, "I am paying for the six cars behind me". The woman had read a card taped to her friend's refrigerator that said, "Practise random acts of kindness and senseless acts of beauty."

Another woman spotted the phrase painted on a warehouse wall and wrote it down. She liked it so much she told her family. Her husband loved it too. He put it up in the classroom for his seventh graders to read. One of his students was the daughter of a local columnist, she told her mum and she put it in the paper.

The phrase spread. It is now on bumper stickers and I've seen it on the noticeboard of a local church. Some people have it on their business cards. A woman in Boston writes Merry Christmas on her cheques. A Sydney couple I know write thank you on their cheques whenever they pay their bills. What can you do?

Senseless acts of kindness spread joy. You can't be kind without feeling better yourself.

The majority of people are nice, kind and honest. But unfortunately the stresses and struggles of daily living sometimes makes you forget this. When you act like the person you want to be, even if you are not quite there yet, you make the world a nicer place to live in. You can't be happy without making others happy. You make the world a better place by sharing your riches with others.

In order to be, you do

Doing means living your purpose, doing for yourself and others all that you aspire to. What is your life all about? Ask yourself these questions:

If I knew I could have everything, what would I do with my time?

What do I want to leave of value when I die, to say that I made a contribution?

What dreams would I pursue if I knew I could not fail?

Dreams are what lead us to our destiny. Dreams enrich our lives and take us beyond mediocrity to passion and fulfilment. Are you being honest with yourself about what you really want?

Scott Alexander[3] says:

Mere wishing or a faint hope is not enough. Most people can't get a burning desire for a dream because their dream is not big enough to create goosebumps, or else they do not believe that they are capable of achieving that dream.

You can have no inner peace as long as the controls of your life are located outside yourself.

Wayne Dyer

If you don't go for it you will never know. Give yourself permission to have all that you want. Act on those desires. Keep your dreams to yourself.

Having it all

Having comes when you acquire the assets that will provide you with the lifestyle, comfort and possessions that you value.

While many fantasise very few reach this level. Fantasies are not dreams. They lack the power and the direction of dreams. Fantasies are what people have when they don't believe that they can have what they really want.

Having is more than the acquisition of material possessions and comfort, as nice as those are. Having is the freedom to live your life the way you choose. Having is sharing your life with those you love. Having is being grateful for all of the blessings that we are surrounded by everyday.

I hear so many people moan about their circumstances and the lack in their life yet they can walk, talk, hear, see, taste, smell, enjoy. Most people in Australia drive a car and have a roof over their head. Look around you at all the blessings that you have and don't wait until it is too late to appreciate just how fortunate you are.

Being the person you want to be and living the life that you want is not just a destination that you arrive at some day and say, Wow! *my life is perfect*. It is a process. You don't have to wait until you have it all - you begin where you are at this moment in time.

Wealth tip:

Once you master money it will no longer control your decisions and choices.

It may take time to acquire the assets and wealth that will ultimately provide you with the lifestyle that you desire, but that does not mean that you have to wait to enjoy it all. Many of life's pleasures are free such as time spent with people whose company you enjoy, walking in a beautiful area, the beauty of nature, libraries are filled with priceless treasures. Ideas, knowledge, kindness and love cannot be bought and can enrich your life today.

Having a plan will get you where you want to go, but a plan is not the be all and end all. Plans will change as you change. Remind yourself that you are in charge of your life and you have the freedom to adapt and change at any time. Ensure that your plans will grow as you grow.

This is your life. Live it to the fullest without stepping on other people's toes and without stepping on your own through negative thoughts. Live creatively, refuse to merely exist. You do this when you concentrate with courage and love on what you want to do. When you nurture the good in you. When you encourage others and when you live life one day at a time while seeking to constantly improve. This is your life and your life is what you make it.

Ultimately your life is what you choose it to be. Choose happiness. Think abundance. Plan for wealth and share it with others.

In Summary

1. Be the person you want to be now.

2. Do the things you want to do now.

3. Practise random acts of kindness and senseless acts of beauty.

4. Be grateful for all that you have now.

5. Choose to be happy.

6. Plan for abundance.

There are risks and costs to a programme of action, but they are far less than the long-range risks and costs of comfortable inaction.

John F Kennedy

Conclusion

Today is the start of the rest of your life

We have come a long way together and I have really enjoyed sharing these ideas with you. How much further you will go will be your decision. This book has given you tools and skills that can change your life, techniques for you to be rich and happy on your income and ideas to assist you to increase your income and build wealth. What you do with these tools is now up to you.

When you put this book down, you can feel that you have learned something and go on as you have always done. Or, you can make a concerted effort to take control of your life, your mind and your finances. You can create powerful beliefs that will produce true wealth for you and the people you care about. But it will only happen if you make it happen.

I have been privileged to share the stage with Stuart Moore who says:

If you do nothing, nothing will happen.

If you do something, something will happen.

The worst that can happen is that you might finish with nothing, which is what you started with.

Therefore, there is really nothing to lose.

There is however, a wonderful opportunity to have a rich and fulfilling life.

Investments come and go, markets go up and down, economies improve and decline. The world is always offering you opportunities of a lifetime, every day of your life, if you choose to see them. They are there. The more the world changes and the more technology changes, the more opportunities you will have to become financially secure.

I want to encourage you to leave the past behind and to welcome change. Go with the flow and sharpen your financial intelligence through research and ongoing education. As a result of the changes, some people will be on their knees, begging for their jobs. Others meanwhile, will accept the challenges and turn lifes curved balls into millions. What will you be doing?

With each dollar coin that comes into your life, you have the power to determine your destiny. Spend it foolishly and you are choosing to be poor. Invest it in your mind by learning how to acquire and manage assets and you are choosing a wealthy future. The choice is yours and only yours. Every day and with every dollar, you decide to be rich or poor.

Today is the start of the rest of your life.

Wherever you are in your life now, is the right place to start. The actions you take today will make the difference. Please write to tell me how you've used what you've learned here to improve your own and others' lives.

"May the road rise to meet you. May the wind be always at your back. May the sun shine warm on your face, may the rains fall soft upon your fields, and until we meet again… may God hold you softly in the palm of His hand."

– Old Irish *blessing*

I wish you wealth and much happiness with this fabulous gift called life.

Hans Jakobi

About the Author

Hans Jakobi

Hans Jakobi is an educator, author and public speaker. He is a chartered accountant by training with a degree in economics and accounting. He is a successful investor and a business entrepreneur who has built several very profitable businesses himself.

Hans is passionate about investing and loves teaching the principles of the money game. His personal mission is: To live and teach the principles of true wealth.

"The main reason people struggle financially is that they haven't learnt the principles of creating wealth. The result is that people learn to work for money but not how to make money work for them" Hans says.

With his unique blend of simplicity, practicality, excitement and humour Hans delivers down-to-earth wealth creation and money management seminars and workshops.

Known to many as the "Million Dollar Man", he is the author of several books including, *How Real Estate Investment Can Work For You*. He is the presenter of the *Wealth Talk*™ Audio Library, the *Super Secrets to Wealth*™ and *Super Secrets to Riches*™, home study courses. Hans publishes the *Super Secrets Newsletter*.

To book Hans to speak for your organisation you can contact him at:
Wealth Dynamics International Pty Ltd
PO Box 86
Illawong NSW 2234
Australia
Telephone: 02 9543 2966
Fax: 02 9543 5048
Email: seminars@supersecrets.com
Internet: www.supersecrets.com

Feedback form

We would love to hear your feedback. If you have had some successful results, no matter how big or small, we would love to hear about them.

What I liked most about *How To Be Rich And Happy On Your Income* was.

_____

_____

_____

_____

Here is what I have decided to do as a result of reading *How To Be Rich And Happy On Your Income*. _____

_____

_____

_____

Here is what I think you can do to improve *How To Be Rich And Happy On Your Income*. _____

_____

_____

_____

Please indicate your wishes below:

☐ Please keep this response confidential ☐ You may publish my comments in future editions of your book or in your promotional material.

Name _____

Address _____

_____ Postcode _____

Phone _____ Fax _____

Email _____

Fax to: 02 9543 5048 or **mail to**: Wealth Dynamics International Pty Ltd PO Box 86 Illawong NSW 2234 Australia

You can visit us on the web at www.supersecrets.com.
Take a look some time and let us know what you think.

Financial terminology

All ordinaries index. A share-market index calculated using the current price of over 300 Australian companies listed on the stock exchange. The All Ordinaries index is used as a guide to how the stockmarket is performing.

Annuities. An investment that you buy that returns you a guaranteed income for a set number of years or for life. There are tax advantages to purchasing annuities.

Assessable income. Your gross income before allowable deductions.

Assets. What you own. I like Robert Kiyosaki's definition of an asset as something that feeds me.

Balance Sheet. A company's bill of health showing the nature and amount of assets and liabilities.

Bank bills. Short term investments for terms up to six months. Usually purchased with amounts of $100,000 plus. Considered to be very secure as they are guaranteed by a bank. Usually purchased at a discount.

Bankruptcy. A situation where liabilities exceed realisable assets. Bankruptcy usually results from legal proceedings to recover a debt.

Bear market. A term used to describe a falling share market.

Blue chip shares. Quality shares in companies known for their ability to make a profit in good times or bad. The yield from blue chip shares is often proportionately low.

Bonus issue. The issue of bonus or free shares to existing shareholders.

Broker. A financial intermediary who acts as an agent in the buying and selling of securities or commodities for which he receives a buying or selling commission. Stockbrokers, wool brokers, insurance brokers all act in a similar capacity.

Brokerage. Fee paid to a broker for their services in buying and selling.

Budget. Estimates of revenues and expenditures (incomings and outgoings).

Bull market. A term used to describe a rising sharemarket.

Capital gains tax. Tax that is paid on the growth component of an asset.

Capital growth. The increase in the value of your investment.

Compound interest. Interest paid on capital plus accumulated interest, i.e interest on interest.

Consumer price index. Commonly know as CPI, this is the measure of inflation. A basket of goods and services is used as a measure.

CRAA. An abbreviation for Credit Reference Association of Australia. This association maintains a record of all credit applications made to member organisations within the last five years (in the case of bankruptcy records are held for seven years).

Depreciation. The decrease in the value of an asset.

Discount. When purchasing investments at a discount you actually take your interest in advance. For example if you purchased an investment for $100,000 and the interest was going to be $5,000 you would pay $95,000 and on maturity receive back $100,000. If you invest the interest that you receive in advance this increases your yield.

Equity. The amount of the asset that you own.

Freehold. Usually refers to properties that have no debt attached.

Gearing. When you borrow to invest.

Gross income. The amount of income before tax or deductions.

Income insurance. Ensures your income in the event of you being unable to work due to sickness or accident. It does not cover you if you are unemployed.

Inflation. A measure of the rising cost of goods and services.

Joint tenants. Usually refers to investments that are owned by one or more people. Any investment owned by joint tenants automatically reverts to the surviving tenant/s upon death.

Leverage. An investment is leveraged when you use a small amount of money and borrow the remainder to hold a much larger investment.

Liabilities. What you owe.

Liquidity. Assets that can easily be converted to cash.

Market value. The current price that the market will pay for an asset.

Mortgage. The holder of a mortgage has the right to sell an asset and has first claim if payments are not made.

Negative gearing. When the tax deductible cost of servicing a loan exceeds the income earned from an asset, it is considered negatively geared.

Net income. The amount of income you receive after tax has been deducted.

Net worth. The amount that your assets are worth after subtracting all liabilities.

Taxable income. The income that you pay tax on after all deductions have been allowed for.

Tax rebate. An amount which is subtracted from tax payable.

Tenants-in-common. Where two or more people own an investment. In the event of death, the share of their investment passes to the beneficiaries nominated in the owner's will.

Term life insurance. Insures the life of the person nominated. This is only paid in the event of death.

Title. The document by which ownership is recorded.

Yield. The actual rate of return obtained from an investment.

Bibliography

1. Terry Braverman, When The Going Gets Tough, The Tough Lighten Up! Mental Floss Publications, Los Angeles USA, 1997.

2. Anne Hartley, Debt Free, Doubleday, Sydney, 1992.

3. Scott Alexander, Rhinoceros Success, Success Centre, Balwyn Vic, 1980.

4. Robert Kiyosaki, Rich Dad, Poor Dad, Tech Press Inc, Arizona USA, 1997.

5. Jack Canfield & Mark Victor Hansen, A 2nd Helping Of Chicken Soup for the Soul, Health Communications, Deerfield Beach, Florida, 1993.

6. Anne Hartley, Psychology of Money, Hart Publishing, Sydney, 1995.

7. Marianne Williamson, A Return to Love, Harper Collins, New York, 1992.

8. Software For The Brain, Dr Michael Hewitt Gleeson, Wrightbooks, North Brighton, Victoria 1989.

9. Goodbye Wage Slave, Belinda Gibbon, Sydney Morning Herald, November 1997.

10. Barbara Sher, I Could Do Anything If I Only Knew What It Was, Hodder & Stoughton, Rydalmere, Sydney 1995.

11. Wayne Dyer, Your Sacred Self, Harper Collins, Pymble, 1995.

12. Conversations with God, Neale Donald Walsch, Hodder & Stoughton, Rydalmere, Sydney 1996.

13. Cyndi Kaplan, Awaken Your Business Creativity, Millenium, Alexandria, 1995.

14. Faith Popcorn, Clicking, Harper Collins, London, 1996.

15. Paul and Sarah Edwards, Finding Your Perfect Work, Tarcher Putnam, New York, 1996.

16. Wayne Dyer, You'll See It When You Believe It, Schwartz Publishing, Melbourne, 1989.

17. Teaching Kids Saving Graces, Justine Trueman, Sydney Morning Herald, April 30, 1997.

18. Choice Magazine, Sydney, January/February 1998.

19. Robert G. Allen, Nothing Down For The Nineties, Simon & Schuster, New York, 1990.

References

George S. Clason, The Richest Man In Babylon, Penguin Books, New York, USA, 1988

Lindsay Cook, The Money Diet, Fontana, London, 1986.

Stephen R. Covey, The Seven Habits Of Highly Effective People, Simon & Schuster, New York, USA, 1989

Viktor Frankl, Man's Search For Meaning, Pocket Books, New York, USA, 1984.

Michael E Gerber, The E Myth Revisited, Harper Collins, New York, 1995.

Napoleon Hill, Think and Grow Rich, Fawcett Publications, Greenwich, 1963.

Frank Newman & Dr Muriel Newman, The Seven Ways To Wealth, Harper Collins, Sydney 1995.

Bob Proctor, You Were Born Rich, Mc Crary Publishing Inc., Willowdale, Ontario, Canada, 1984

Sterling W Sill, How To Personally Profit From The Laws Of Success, National Institute of Financial Planning, Inc. Salt Lake City, USA, 1984.

Larry Walsch, The Complete Idiot's Guide To Getting Rich, Alpha books, New York.

Index

How To Keep Building On The Information You Have Learnt In This Book

Wealth Dynamics International provides investment education, coaching and consulting services. One of your keys to success is to constantly improve your financial competence. You can do this by regularly consulting your investment reference library and keeping it up to date. It is our objective to support you in this mission and therefore we have created The Wealth Library Club.

The Wealth Library Club
A Continuing Education and Motivation Programme
The Mission Statement for The Wealth Library Club

The Mission of The Wealth Library Club is to provide practical, enjoyable and powerful books, tapes, reports, magazines and courses of the highest calibre. This material will educate and motivate members to ~ attain financial independence, to achieve mastery of important business knowledge, to improve their interpersonal skills and other such related entrepreneurial and life abilities.

The recommended reference library materials change all the time.

To join The Wealth Library Club write, phone, fax or email our office to receive details of the latest material.

Wealth Dynamics International Pty Ltd
PO Box 86
Illawong NSW 2234 Australia
Telephone: (02) 9543 2966
Fax: (02) 9543 5048
Email: wealth@supersecrets.com
Website: http://www.supersecrets.com

Wealth Dynamics
INTERNATIONAL PTY LTD

Now you can listen to interesting people share their tips, ideas and specialised knowledge on the Wealth Talk Audio Library.

Wealth Talk Audios allow you to make productive use of that time which you would otherwise waste in traffic. To order, simply mark your selection in front of each tape title. The following tapes are available as part of this series:

☐ Dynamic Self Managed Super Fund Strategies featuring David Wolrige

Do you want to know how to make your Super Fund work for you now as well as when you retire? The truth is, you need to know as much as you possibly can about superannuation. Wouldn't you like to have the advantage of knowing how superannuation can work for you now? How you can make real money, enjoy substantial tax savings and utilise your previously locked up capital. You'll discover the answers to these questions and more on this tape.

☐ Offshore Investment Strategies featuring Lance Spicer

Have you ever wondered why celebrities, millionaires and major corporations live or set up financial structures in places like Bermuda, the Carribean, the Channel Islands and other exotic places? Because they save money and lots of it. How do they do it? Lance Spicer will reveal exactly how it's done and why it will work for you too! Lance Spicer is an accountant and author of many books and reports on the subject of offshore investment strategies and has access to some amazing investment opportunities offshore. Some of his information has been described as "the information your government doesn't want you to know!"

☐ The Wealth Accelerator Programme featuring Karyn Graham

On this tape you'll discover how to cut 17 years off the term of your mortgage; how to eliminate tens of thousands of dollars in mortgage interest and how to build home equity faster. Karyn also tells you how you can create "Money Magic" so that you'll never need to ask your bank manager for a loan again. She developed the Wealth Accelerator Programme to give you the security of owning your family home sooner than you thought possible, - without changing your lifestyle.

☐ Creating Wealth Through Real Estate Investment featuring Kevin Taylor

Real estate has a long and successful history of investment performance with minimal risk. One of its outstanding features is capital growth, or the potential of increasing property values. This characteristic about property has allowed many Australians to increase their net worth over time with minimal effort. Can you still make money in Real Estate today? How can you buy property without using your own cash? Can you save taxes legitimately by investing in property? You'll discover the answers to these and other questions on this interesting tape with Kevin Taylor.

☐ Property Conveyancing Made Simple featuring Paul Denny

When you buy or sell a property you are probably undertaking one of the biggest financial transactions of your life. Because of the complex and comprehensive legal requirements of these transactions, the financial consequences of a mistake or an oversight can be devastating. On this tape, Paul Denny explains how you can protect yourself when buying and selling property. Paul Denny is a professional specialist property conveyancer with over 20 years experience. He also explains how you can minimise your land tax exposure and he explains the steps involved in the actual conveyancing process. If you're buying or selling property (or thinking about it) you really need to order Paul Denny's tape.

☐ The Keys to Successful Property Management featuring John Marriott

To be a successful landlord, you need to have your property well managed. One of the most important aspects that effect property's return is the ongoing management and the security of the rental income. Selecting exceptional tenants willing to maintain your most valuable asset, is crucial. Equally, the selection of a professional Property Manager is essential. This ensures your financial security, and gives you peace of mind as an investor. On this tape John will explain how you can be a "headache free" landlord.

Each single tape is $25 plus $4 postage and packing.

Here are some other great Business, Success and Money Books to add to your self-improvement library. Now conveniently available by mail order. Simply mark your selection in front of each title and complete the coupon below.

☐ **The Psychology of Money -
How to turn your dreams into reality**
by Anne Hartley, Author of "Financially Free"
$20

Discover the secrets of prosperous people. This
book is full of inspirational stories about real
people who have achieved their dreams. This
book will not only inspire you, it will show
you clearly and practically, how to create the
life you want.

☐ **The Australian Share Market Guide**
by Lance Spicer
$49.50

This book will show you how to earn a good
living from investing and trading shares on
the stockmarket like a professional. By
using the buy and sell indicators
recommended in this book, you will
learn how to take much of the risk out of
share market investment

☐ **Be Seen, Get Known, Move Ahead**
by Robyn Henderson
$25

The leading edge beginner's guide to self
promotion. Everything you wanted to know
about building your career and business and
didn't know who to ask.

☐ **Networking for $uccess**
by Robyn Henderson
$25

This Ultimate Networking guide takes you
on a "how to" journey from exchanging
business cards, to building rapport, to
writing. A must for everyone in business or
wanting to be in business. Ideas packed!

☐ **The Magic Of Networking**
2 Pack Audio Programme
with Robyn Henderson
$95

This live presentation shows you how to
improve your networking skills &
implement simple daily/weekly strategies
to maximise your networking efforts.

FREE NEWSLETTER

Return this Form now for a FREE Super Secrets Newsletter Subscription

Imagine… 12 months worth of Australia's best wealth creation strategies and *do-it-yourself* investment ideas delivered to your doorstep every three months…for **FREE.** Just complete the form below with your contact details telling us you would love a **FREE** 12 months subscription to The Super Secrets Newsletter valued at A$199. This is a limited offer to readers of this book only. To make sure you receive your newsletter…please complete this form immediately.

Each edition of The Super Secrets Newsletter is packed with simple strategies for *do-it-yourself* wealth creation. You'll find articles from Hans and other guest writers on how to save money, invest sensibly and protect your assets wisely. You'll also find stories telling how people just like you have overcome the odds and started on the path to financial freedom. Send today for your free subscription.

To

Reply Paid 5

Wealth Dynamics International Pty Ltd

PO Box 86

Illawong NSW 2234

Australia

YES Please register me for a FREE 12 month subscription to The Super Secrets Newsletter. Would you also please send me information about the other items I have ticked.

☐ I'd like to know more about Hans Jakobi's seminars and workshops

☐ Please send me information about the Super Secrets to Wealth Home Study Course

☐ Please send me details about your other products and services

We would appreciate knowing how you discovered this book.

☐ Bookstore..............   ☐ Newspaper/magazine

☐ Friend/associate   ☐ Direct mail

☐ Gift   ☐ My company

☐ Radio/television   ☐ Other..........................

Age and Income

☐ 25 & under   ☐ 26-45   ☐ 46-65   ☐ 65+

☐ $0-35,000   ☐ $35,001-$75,000   ☐ $75,000+

My details are as follows:

Name _____

Address _____

_____ Postcode _____

Home Ph. _____ Work Ph. _____

Fax _____ E-Mail _____